Of Earth and Little Rain

Of Earth
and Little Rain

THE PAPAGO INDIANS

Bernard L. Fontana

Photographs by John P. Schaefer

THE UNIVERSITY OF ARIZONA PRESS   TUCSON

THE UNIVERSITY OF ARIZONA PRESS

Copyright © 1989
The Arizona Board of Regents
All Rights Reserved

Manufactured in the United States of America
∞ This book is printed on acid-free, archival-quality paper.
93 92 91 90 89   5 4 3 2 1

Library of Congress Cataloging-in-Publication Data

Fontana, Bernard L.
Of earth and little rain   :   the Papago Indians /
by Bernard L. Fontana;
with photographs by John P. Schaefer.
p.   cm.
Reprint. Originally published: Flagstaff, Ariz.,
Northland Press, © 1981.
ISBN 0-8165-1146-2 (alk. paper)
1. Tohono O'Odham Indians.   I. Schaefer, John Paul, 1934–
II. Title.
E99.P25F66   1989   89-5225
979.1'004974 – dc20   CIP

British Library Cataloguing in Publication data are available.

Originally published by the Northland Press in 1981

For Ruth M. Underhill and Daniel S. Matson,
who learned the secret of Papago songs

Since this volume was first issued in 1981, the Arizona people formerly known as Papago Indians have officially changed their name to Tohono O'odham (Desert People). The change was adopted as part of a new constitution approved by members of the Tohono O'odham Nation (formerly the Papago Indian Tribe of Arizona) in January 1986.

Although some of the photos here were included in the earlier book, many others have been selected for this reissue.

Contents

Acknowledgments

Were it not for the generosity of Byron Ivancovich, publication of this book would not have been possible. Since 1955 Byron has encouraged the author to pursue his curiosity in matters connected with Spanish colonial history and Papago Indians, and more recently he has manifested his strong support for the art of photography. Our mutual debt to him is one impossible to repay.

We will also be unable to repay our debt to Danny Lopez, who accompanied us on many trips on both sides of the international boundary. We further express our gratitude to other Papagos who extended their kindness to us: Ascencio Antone, Laura Antone, Fillman Bell, Rafael García V., Laura Kermen, Clara Lopez, Juan Lopez, Ramon Lopez, Luciano Noriego, Margaret Ortega, Philip Salcido, David Santos, and Ofelia Zepeda.

Finally, we wish to thank others who offered information or who helped in various ways: Fernando Castañeda, former Director of the Residencia Pápagos of Mexico's Instituto Nacional Indigenista; Fr. Celestine Chinn, O.F.M.; James Enyeart, Director of the Center for Creative Photography; Fr. Lambert Fremdling, O.F.M.; James S. Griffith, Director of the Southwest Folklore Center; Emil W. Haury; Gordon Krutz; Fr. Kieran McCarty, O.F.M.; Daniel S. Matson; Pablo Miranda of Caborca, Sonora; James E. Officer; the Polaroid Corporation; Fr. Regis Rohder, O.F.M.; and Rosa María Vicencio Estrada, an anthropologist with the Instituto Nacional Indigenista. Too, we thank the members of our respective families who tolerated our absences from home while we toured the Papaguería.

B.L.F.
J.P.S.

Preface

They call themselves O'odham. The word means "People,"
but it means more than that. It also means Those Who
Emerged from the Earth. It means sand, or dry earth, en-
dowed with human quality. The O'odham, or Papagos, as
we call them, are of the earth. But it is of earth in a land of
little rain. That is their essence. It is the secret of their life.
They are the desert people.

If we think it quaint that Papagos are of the earth, we
betray an ignorance of our own traditions. The Judeo-
Christian Adam, our first man, takes his name from the

Hebrew *adhamah* (earth). Nor is it a linguistic accident that "human" and "humus" share the same ultimate Indo-European meaning: earth. So Papagos and the rest of humankind have a common origin. But the soil from which O'odham culture sprang was comparatively dry. Perhaps this helps account for the reason they have retained their sense of humanity and of related humility better than we. They remain close to their roots when most of us have departed from ours.

This book is meant to provide an appreciation, in words and photographs, of one of the lesser-known groups of Indians in the United States and Mexico. That they are so little known to outsiders despite the fact that their reservation is the second largest in the United States says something about the depth of their humility. It also says something about the average Papago's sense of self because, in reality, the average Papago sees no point in being "public like a frog." He knows what Edgar Allan Poe knew, that fame is a food that dead men eat.

If Papagos are generally indifferent about being well known to others, they are not indifferent to the need all human beings share for sympathetic understanding. For better or for worse, we are neighbors on the globe. If we are to be good neighbors, we must be able to see one another beyond the confines of culturally induced myopia. As our understanding of others deepens, so does our understanding of ourselves. There is truth in ancient wisdom: "We are in them and they are in us."

For twenty-five years the author of this volume has lived with his family about fifteen feet from the western edge of the San Xavier Papago Indian Reservation. He has studied Papago history and culture throughout those years; he was the Papago Tribe's expert witness in its successfully prosecuted claims case against the United States government. Much of the material in this book, though, including all of the photographs, is the result of several trips made by author and photographer together throughout 1979 and 1980. For the photographer, these trips provided a first in-depth look at most of the Papaguería. For the author, they were a refresher course, including a few visits to places he had not seen for fifteen to twenty years. The forays — always by automobile — to Sonoran Papago country were new to both of us.

Those who have perused our earlier book, *Tarahumara: Where Night Is the Day of the Moon* (Flagstaff: Northland Press, 1979), will immediately perceive that the modern situation for Papago Indians and Tarahumara Indians is quite different. Many Tarahumaras are still living in a subsistence economy; Papagos are inextricably involved in the cash economy and industrial society of the western world. To know the Tarahumaras of today is to know the Papagos of a hundred years ago; to know the Papagos of today is perhaps to know what future generations of Tarahumaras have in store for them. There are other differences, many of them obvious, between these two groups as well. Less obvious are the many similarities. Most outstanding among them is the fact that both groups persist as clearly identifiable cultural entities in the face of tremendous pressures by the outside world to assimilate them. Each group survives in its own way. It is likely that this book will be written and these photographs taken — with different text and different scenes — a hundred years hence. There will still be Papagos, and posterity will be the richer for it.

Bernard L. Fontana
John P. Schaefer

The University of Arizona
Tucson
1980

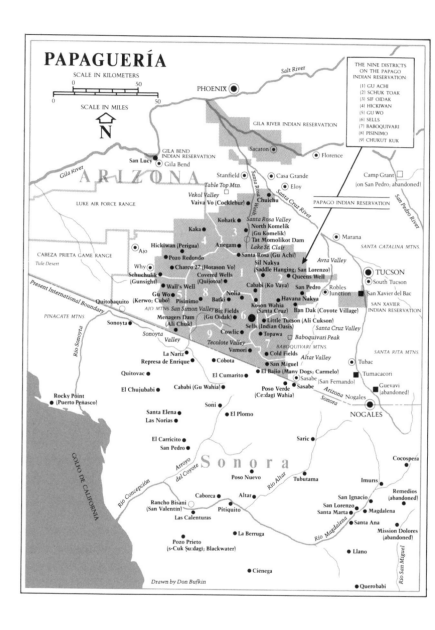

PAPAGUERÍA

SCALE IN KILOMETERS
0   50

0   50
SCALE IN MILES

N

THE NINE DISTRICTS
ON THE PAPAGO
INDIAN RESERVATION:
(1) GU ACHI
(2) SCHUK TOAK
(3) SIF OIDAK
(4) HICKIWAN
(5) GU WO
(6) SELLS
(7) BABOQUIVARI
(8) PISINIMO
(9) CHUKUT KUK

Salt River

PHOENIX ●

GILA RIVER INDIAN RESERVATION

Sacaton ●

● Florence

GILA BEND
INDIAN RESERVATION
San Lucy ●   ● Gila Bend

Gila River

A R I Z O N A

Camp Grant □
(on San Pedro; abandoned)

PAPAGO INDIAN RESERVATION

San Pedro River

LUKE AIR FORCE RANGE

Stanfield ●   ● Casa Grande
Table Top Mtn. □
Vekol Valley □   ● Eloy
Vaiva Vo (Cocklebur) ●

Chuichu ●

Santa Rosa Wash
Santa Cruz River

Kohatk ●
Kaka ●   North Komelik
          (Gu Komelik)
          Tat Momolikot Dam
Anegam ● Lake St. Clair

Santa Rosa Valley

● Marana

SANTA CATALINA MTNS.

CABEZA PRIETA GAME RANGE
Tule Desert

Hickiwan (Perigua) ●
● Ajo
● Pozo Redondo

Santa Rosa (Gu Achi) ●
Sil Nakya
(Saddle Hanging; San Lorenzo)
Queens Well

Avra Valley

● TUCSON

Why ●   ● Charco 27 (Hotason Vo)
Schuchulik ●   Covered Wells
(Gunsight)   (Quijotoa)
        Wall's Well ●
Gu Wo ●   Nolia ●
(Kerwo; Cubo) Pisinimo ● Batki ●
Quitobaquito ●   AJO MTNS. San Simon Valley Big Fields
Menagers Dam ● (Gu Oidak)
(Ali Chuk)
Sonoyta ●

Cababi (Ko Vaya)
San Pedro ● Robles
          Junction

● South Tucson

■ San Xavier del Bac

Koson Wahia   Ban Dak (Coyote Village)
(Santa Cruz)
● Little Tucson (Ali Cukson)
Sells (Indian Oasis)
Topawa ●

Havana Nakya

SAN XAVIER
INDIAN RESERVATION

Santa Cruz Valley

Present International Boundary

PINACATE MTNS.

Sonoyta
Valley

Cowlic ●
Tecolote Valley
La Nariz ●   Vamori ●
Represa de Enrique ●   ● Cobota
Quitovac ●
       El Cumarito ●
El Chujubabi ●   Cababi (Gu Wahia) ●

□ Baboquivari Peak
BABOQUIVARI MTNS.
Cold Fields ●   Altar Valley
● San Miguel

● El Bajío (Many Dogs; Carmelo)
● Sasabe (San Fernando)
Poso Verde   Sasabe ●
(Ce:dagi Wahia)

SANTA RITA MTNS.

● Tubac

Arizona
Sonora

■ Tumacacori

Guevavi
(abandoned) ■

● Nogales

Soni ●
Santa Elena ●
Las Norias ●

● El Plomo

NOGALES ●

El Carricito ●
San Pedro ●

● Saric

S o n o r a

Cocospera ●

Arroyo
del Coyote

Rio Concepción

Poso Nuevo ●

Rio Altar

Tubutama ●

Imuris ●

Remedios
(abandoned) ●

GOLFO DE CALIFORNIA

Rocky Point
● (Puerto Peñasco)

Caborca ●   Altar ●
Rancho Bisani ●
(San Valentín)   Pitiquito ●
Las Calenturas

San Ignacio ●
San Lorenzo ●
Santa Marta ● Magdalena ●

Rio Magdalena

● Santa Ana

Mission Dolores
(abandoned) ■

● La Berruga

● Llano

Pozo Prieto
(s-Cuk Su:dagi; Blackwater)

Rio San Miguel

● Ciénega

● Querobabi

Drawn by Don Bufkin

Antonio

A PROLOGUE

Antonio Reyes, Papago Indian, was our neighbor. The first time we saw him was one very dark autumn night when he stood on our front porch holding a flashlight. I opened the door when he knocked and invited him in. He was a short, stocky man, slightly hunched over in a typical elderly Papago stance with his legs in parentheses, a sure sign of years in the saddle, rounding up cattle or simply getting from place to place. The black hair of his youth touched with traces of grey belied his age, about sixty-two or sixty-three, I should guess. He was, even so — as my wife Hazel pointed out to me more than once — a very handsome man.

Antonio was a little uneasy that first visit. I offered him a seat on our couch, and he sat there for some time before he took off his broad-brimmed hat and relaxed. But then, old-fashioned Papagos think it is impolite to take off one's hat in someone else's house, especially in the house of a stranger. We feel the same way about shoes.

I can no longer remember what it was we talked about that evening. It wasn't much. There were long, but not anxious, silences between the sentences of conversation. Hazel brought in coffee and cake. We sipped the coffee, nibbled at the cake, and spoke occasionally in hushed voices. It was a cold night, and Antonio seemed to be enjoying the heat of our wood-burning stove. At long last he got around to the point of his visit. He wanted to go to town to shop the next morning, and he wondered if we would give him a ride. All Souls' Day was near. Antonio wanted to buy some candles, crêpe paper, and flowers so he could decorate the graves of his friends and relatives who were lying in the San Xavier cemetery. We said we'd be glad to take him, and shortly after that I drove him home across the road, letting him out in front of his little two-room adobe house.

In the morning Antonio was waiting for us by the mailboxes on the road, and we took him to town. We also took his daughter, Carmen, a chubby girl about fourteen years old. No one said much as we drove along until we were halfway there.

"What time are you coming back out?" asked Antonio.

"I don't know," I lied. "Why?"

"We'll be through about twelve o'clock."

"Do you need a ride?"

"That's what we were thinking. We could use a ride back home."

"Okay. I'll pick you up at the bus depot about noon. I'll be glad to bring you back out." And this time I wasn't lying.

We saw a lot of Antonio and his daughter Carmen after that. We took them into town almost every Saturday morning, and almost every Saturday I would make a special trip later to bring them back home. They came over often during the week, too, visiting with us for two or three hours. Carmen sat on the couch and read the public records section of the newspaper and looked at pictures in magazines while Antonio and Hazel and I talked. We gossiped about the other people in the village—never maliciously, because Antonio would never have stood for it. We talked about Antonio's family background; we talked about world affairs. One night he saw a picture of a guided missile on the front page of the newspaper.

"What's that?" he wanted to know.

"That's a guided missile," I said. "They're building them to put bombs in them for war. And they're even trying to make one that will go to the moon."

Antonio chuckled. Or at least he smiled. "Go to the moon?" He smiled again. Then thoughtful silence. "Let them go."

Little by little the story of Antonio Reyes began to unfold. He had been born at San Xavier, but when he was young he moved to the village of Coyote Sits on the "Big Reservation." He married there and had a son, Aloysius, and then a daughter, Carmen. His wife died when Carmen was only three. The job of raising a young daughter and a son became Antonio's lot, and with the help of some old women in Coyote Sits who spoke only Papago, he succeeded admirably. When Aloysius was old enough, he went away to the Indian boarding school at Riverside, California. And when Carmen finished grammar school on the Big Reservation, Antonio brought her back to San Xavier where she could go to a public junior high school, and also where she could get her hearing treated by an ear specialist in Tucson. Her hearing was very poor.

Antonio's brother, Simon, lived with him and Carmen in the little house across the road. Simon had served in the infantry in World War II, and Antonio was very proud of him—despite the fact that his brother was inclined to tipple more than he should. "I don't know why they put him in jail," Antonio would say. "He was just having a little fun." Antonio didn't drink liquor at all.

His greatest loves in life were his two children. His son wrote him letters regularly. Simon had worked in Yosemite National Park one year, so Hazel and I showed Antonio color slides of Yosemite. He was delighted. He had never been to California, nor had he ever been beyond the Papaguería, for that matter. He had been a desert dweller all his life, working hard to make a living from the few cattle he raised and from an occasional cotton crop.

Many were the warm and pleasant evenings we four spent together. We would often show color slides—of Alaska, of Illinois, California, northern Arizona. But the ones he and Carmen liked best were those of southern Arizona, of home, of Indians, of Mission San Xavier del Bac. They never tired of looking at them, even the same ones over and over.

And later I began to pull out books and manuscripts about Papago Indians. Antonio and I would sit on the couch together, and he would laugh as he read the material, correcting this point or that point as he saw fit, or saying, "That sure is the way it is." It amused him that things Papago had been written down. He was tolerant of my interest and even volunteered to teach me the language. "If you can write it down," he would say, "you won't have any trouble learning it."

I remember one night when I showed him an earthenware Papago effigy. It was a white pot in the shape of a hooked-nose man whose clothes were outlined in black paint. "Is that I'itoi (the Papagos' mythical culture hero)?" I asked him.

He put the vessel in his hand, looked at it a moment, and smiled. "It looks like George Washington," he said. And, indeed, it did.

Antonio was everything anthropology books about Papagos say they are supposed to be. He was kind and generous. He dearly loved his children; he was honest to a fault; and he had a quick wit and a perceptive mind and insight. He was entitled to money from the American Smelting & Refining Company for a copper lease, for

4

example, but he nearly turned it down. He was due the money because his wife's family had owned the land on which the lease was made. The law says that anything belonging to his wife became half his on her death, with the other half divided evenly between their two children. But Papago tradition with respect to inheritance is not identical. To Antonio's way of thinking, any land that had belonged to his wife still belonged to her family of birth and not to him. It was only with much persuading and appealing to him to think about the future of his children that he finally claimed the money, about $3,000, that was his due. And at that, he drew out only $100.

It was about 9:30 one Saturday night, and I was in our bathroom painting the walls with white enamel paint. There was a knock at the front door, and in a minute Hazel came to say that Antonio wanted to see me. I walked into the living room, paint bucket in one hand and brush in the other, with daubs of paint smeared on my face and clothes.

"Are you busy?" Antonio wanted to know.

"A little bit, Antonio. I'm trying to finish painting our bathroom."

"Oh," he said.

"What can I do for you?" I asked, more than a little exasperated.

"Well, it seems like the girls, Carmen and her girl friend, have left."

"Where did they go, Antonio?"

"That's just it. I don't know. They went out into the desert somewhere."

"What can I do?" I wanted to know. "Is there anything I can do to help?"

"That's what I thought. Maybe you could help. Seems like Jerome Lewis came over, and he's pretty drunk. Wouldn't be so bad, but he's making a lot of noise. And that's what the girls didn't like. He won't go to sleep or it would be all right. But he keeps making all that noise, so the girls got mad and left for somewhere."

"What do you want me to do?"

"Well, I thought maybe you could come over in your

pickup and that we could put him in it and take him home. I wouldn't care if he would fall asleep, but if I don't get him out of the house the girls won't come back."

I put down the bucket and brush, washed my hands in paint thinner and soap, put on my coat, and away we went to get Jerome. When we got to Antonio's house, he and his brother and I managed to half drag, half carry Jerome to the cab of my '49 Dodge pickup. He was almost 250 pounds of dead weight, but somehow we managed to stuff him onto the seat. Antonio climbed in alongside of him and off we drove, bouncing over desert roads in the pitch darkness to Jerome's house. When we got there, Antonio and I lifted him out and got him onto his bed. I went back outside and sat in the truck. Inside, Antonio was talking with Jerome's sister—and through the open door I could see Jerome beginning to come back to life. Outside there were women stirring about in the yard and under the *ramada*, lighting fires and getting ready to cook.

The scene was straight from a nineteenth-century past. Here was an unplastered and unpainted two-room, sun-dried adobe house resting in the desert. The wooden door was wide ajar, and light from a flickering kerosene lantern cast human shadows on the wall. A woman inside—and then another who appeared—wore shawls over their heads. A dark-skinned Papago man spoke in earnest while another, coming out of his drunken stupor, sat up on the edge of a single bunk bed. The floor was packed earth. More people began to gather in front of the house; more women arrived to help with the cooking.

I waited almost twenty minutes—a long time, it seemed to me—but not nearly so long as the timeless depths into which I had a sudden and unexpected glimpse that night: Papago Indians on the desert speaking a language that only they can understand, a language that transcends the spoken word.

At last Antonio came out. "Let's go home," I said.

Ignoring my words, he spoke. "Seems like somebody died out here today."

"I'm very sorry, Antonio. But it's getting late. Let's go

back home." He looked at the ground at his feet, then shuffled a little. I weakened. "Is there something we can do?"

He brightened. "That's what I thought. We might help. This man, he died over by the Mission and he's supposed to be over here. I thought we could go and get the body and bring it over here."

I said that we would, and Antonio went back into the house to get Jerome. Jerome, by this time, had sobered considerably. He was able to climb into the pickup's seat under his own power. On the way to a house near the mission, I learned that the dead man—who was some kind of an "uncle" to Jerome—had been living in town for nearly twenty years. He had not, until that very day, set foot on San Xavier home soil in all that time. He had climbed off the bus at six that evening, and twenty minutes later he dropped dead. He had been an alcoholic.

We reached the place where the body was supposed to be, but it was gone. Another shadowy Papago conference revealed that someone had gotten there ahead of us with a horse and wagon and had picked the body up. We started back, driving past the mission.

"He was a Catholic," Antonio volunteered.

"That's right," agreed Jerome. "Drive to the Mission and get Father Celestine. We have to have the last rites."

I dutifully drove to the rear of the mission. I hammered at the gate to the cloister. Old Father Nicholas appeared. I hurriedly explained what had happened. "Was it a violent death?" he asked. I told him I didn't think so. He then took me to Father Celestine's new room.

I offered to drive Father Celestine to the scene, but when he saw how crowded we were, he decided to follow in his own car. When we got back to Jerome's, a large group had gathered, and the wake had gotten under way. The body was lying out in the desert about fifty feet from the house. A kerosene lantern lighted the corpse, its hands folded over its chest and a hat over its face. Father Celestine, diminutive Father Celestine, garbed in the brown habit and hood of a Franciscan priest, performed the last rites there in the dark chill of a desert winter night. When it was over he looked for me among the Papagos. When he found me he pulled the hood back from his head and exclaimed, "How in the world did you get mixed up in this?"

"It's a long story, Father. A long story."

He got in his car and drove away. The mourners moved inside the house to get out of the cold air and to eat the food cooked for the wake. The corpse was left to care for itself under the cactus and creosote bushes. Antonio grabbed me gently by the arm. "Let's go home now," he whispered. So we, too, left.

Several minutes later, I dropped him off in front of his own adobe house. He climbed out of the truck, and just before I pulled away I heard him say, "I hope Hazel won't be too mad."

She wasn't.

One day, about six weeks later, I was working in the front yard when I heard the bells of Mission San Xavier toll the death knell. Bong. Silence. Bong. Silence. Bong . . .

An hour after that, a Papago Indian woman walked into our front yard. There were tears in her eyes. "Did you know about Tony?" she asked.

"Tony who?"

"Tony Reyes." And she sobbed. "He died this morning. I know you are a good friend of his, and I thought you'd like to know."

I told Hazel briefly what had happened before I took this woman, the wife of Antonio's nephew, back to Antonio's house. There must have been nearly a hundred people in the yard. A huge feast was being prepared. Inside the little house lay Antonio, his feet toward the door and a rosary, a beautiful rosary, in the hands folded over his chest. Carmen was there crying disconsolately. I did what I could to help. I hauled tables and chairs for the wake. I hauled water. And when I got home there were tears in Hazel's eyes.

The funeral was two days later. We went early in the morning. Again the church bells rang their mournful song; again we cried. And soon Antonio was being carried in his coffin from the mission, going slowly toward the cemetery where he was to rest forever.

I saw his neighbor, Crispin Pablo, after that. "He was breaking that big brown horse," said Crispin. "I just don't know who's going to break him now."

And neither did I.

Desert

Home is a desert. But not a sandy, treeless waste. Indeed, a visitor in eary spring, provided there have been winter rains, or in August, if summer rainfall has been normal, might wonder why it is called a "desert." Barren, forsaken, and abandoned are not notions appropriate for a region whose floor is carpeted with the green of millions of annual plants. Mesquite, acacia, and ironwood trees are in leaf; long-stemmed cactuses such as saguaro, cardón, senita, and organ pipe are evergreen. So are the prickly pear cactus, cane cactus, creosote bush, paloverde, and bursage.

March in the Gregorian calendar takes its name from Mars, the god of war. Its color, like that of the planet Mars, is the red of human blood. But the same period in the Papago calendar is Ce:dagĭ Masad, "green month [moon]." It is a time to gather the long and narrow leaves of bear grass to be made into baskets. It is a time when desert trees, stark in the random confusion of brown branches and stems empty of leaves, erupt in yellow-green ponchos to interrupt the open vista of level valleys.

The Gregorian and Papago calendars more closely coincide in the last full month of summer. The days labeled in honor of Augustus Caesar, "august" or "majestic," are equally grand in the Sonoran Desert. They are Sopol Esabig Masad (short planting month), when the seeds of corn, squash, and tepary beans must go into the ground lest their blossoms and fruit run the risk of frostbite. If all is well, heavy summer rains have come, and both mountains and intervening plains are their richest green.

The Papago Indians live in the northern portions of the Sonoran Desert. Definitions of the extent of the Sonoran Desert vary, but if one includes the whole of central Baja California, adding it to the arid portions of southwestern Arizona, southeastern California, northeastern Baja California, and virtually all of western Sonora, it is a region of about 120,000 square miles. The Papago range in northwestern Sonora and southwestern Arizona is perhaps one-fifth of that, or some 24,000 square miles. Although there is no accurate way of arriving at a figure for the size of the aboriginal population, some 12,000 is probably a fair guess. The average of one human being per two square miles of northern Sonoran Desert sounds about right for a people who had to coax their entire subsistence from a thirsty surround. The present Papago population of between 13,000 and 16,000 is perhaps as large as it has ever been, and very few, if any, Papagos continue to depend on the desert environment for most of their basic needs.

The Sonoran Desert is the lowest and the hottest of North American deserts. Its varied cactuses and small-leaved vegetation literally march down to the sea where its borders outline the upper half of the Gulf of California. Large expanses of southwesternmost Arizona and northwesternmost Sonora average less than an inch of annual rainfall. Within the total region, however, there is almost infinite variety. Arroyos, which provide the natural drainageways for an infrequent runoff of rain water, are lined with trees and large shrubs. And depending on altitude, latitude, longitude, soils, direction of exposure, and degree of slope, the numbers and kinds of plants and animals change drastically from one locale to another. This "desert" is many little worlds in one.

In the desert region of the aptly labeled Basin and Range Province, mountain ranges and valleys alternate with one another, parallel rows lying generally southeast to northwest and becoming higher above sea level moving from west to east. The Gila and Tinajas Altas mountains, just east of the lower Colorado River boundary between California and Arizona, top out at a mere 3,150 feet. By contrast, the Catalina and Santa Rita ranges walling in the eastern edge of the Sonoran Desert in Arizona rise to more than 9,000 feet. Between these sets of mountains are other "islands in the sky," Kitt Peak (6,882 feet) and Baboquivari Peak (7,730 feet) the most prominent among them. The vegetation on their upper slopes, where rainfall is up to fifteen inches a year, is not that of a desert but consists instead of oak, pinyon, and juniper.

Ascending the staircase from the Colorado River eastward, with the mountains as risers and intermontane valleys as treads, the climb is from the 500-foot-high Yuma Desert to the Santa Cruz Valley at the head of the stairs at about 2,500 feet. Intervening steps are plains with names like Lechuguilla, Mohawk, Tule, Ajo, Sonoyta, Vekol, San Simon, and Avra. The plants growing in each of them are characteristic of the Sonoran Desert.

Above all, what defines a desert is aridity. Water, or its lack, is the great consideration around which life revolves in arid zones. Plant life depends on sunlight, soil, and water; animal life, including the human kind, depends on plant life. Plants in the Sonoran Desert grow in greatest abundance where the soil is right and, above all, where there is the most water. Such places attract the majority of animals. Life therefore reaches its zenith of luxuriance along this desert's riverine perimeters and ephemeral drainageways and in the very few places where there are permanent springs. Historically, as now, man's largest and most concentrated settlements have been along the desert's rivers.

Just as the altitude of the land increases moving from west to east, so does the amount of yearly rainfall. The western one-third of the northern Sonoran Desert has from zero to five inches annually. The central third has from five to ten inches; the eastern third enjoys from ten to fifteen inches. The higher elevations of the mountains everywhere get more rain than the valleys below them.

There are two rainy seasons: summer and winter. Summer storms, called "chubascos" in regional Spanish, reach their greatest intensity in July and August. Moving from east to west from the Gulf of Mexico, they come in the form of scattered black cumulus clouds filled with the power of lightning and the steady rumble and roar of thunder. Such storms are often no more than a mile in diameter, with the result that torrential downpours are highly localized. They move in quickly with their electrifying and drowning force, drench the earth, and pass on to let the summer sun do its drying work before the next storm arrives.

The winter rains, most of which fall in December and January, come from the other direction. They spread in a solid overcast from the Pacific Ocean, moving from west to east. These "equipatas," as they are known to rural Mexicans, lack the devastating force of summer rains. Lightning from such storms is rare; the downfall is slow and steady. On rare occasions the winter rains turn to snow; in the higher elevations they almost inevitably do.

July is a hot month, January, a cold one. Extremes in Yuma, on the lower Colorado River, are 120°F. to 22°F., but with a salubrious 74.5°F. yearly average. Mean temperatures in the central portion of the northern Sonoran Des-

13

ert are 64° to 72°F.; in Tucson, at the eastern edge, they are just a little cooler. Averages, however, mask the real situation. As thousands of tourists and winter visitors have discovered in modern times, the Sonoran Desert boasts a pleasant temperature most of the year, although its extremes can be very uncomfortable. The heat of summer daylight hours begins to build in later April and early May toward the dehydrator conditions of June and early July, interrupted only by nightfall and broken only by the arrival of the summer rains. And while the rains bring relief in lowering the temperature, stark aridity changes to stifling humidity. This is to say nothing of the terror lightning and flash floods can invoke.

Winter, generally balmy, can surprise with its sudden and burning frosts. Nights are especially cold, but even the daytime, with the sun sweeping relatively low across the southern sky, can make the warming presence of a lighted fireplace feel most welcome. Leaves of deciduous trees fall to the earth; insects and reptiles disappear from sight; blankets are a desired addition to one's place of sleep.

Typically, all plant life in the Sonoran Desert, except for that growing in or adjacent to permanent sources of fresh water, is drought resistant. Beyond that, there is enough variety in types and percentages of different kinds of plants that botanists have delineated seven different vegetation zones for the entire region. The boundaries separating them are not rigid, each zone's flora grading off almost imperceptibly into the next. The two northern zones, where the Papago Indians live, are called the Lower Colorado Valley vegetation province and the Arizona Upland vegetation province. The Lower Colorado Valley segment, lying to the west in the lower and drier portions of the desert, is a land of little-leaved plants; creosote bush and bursage account for about eighty-five percent of the plant cover. The remainder is made up of trees such as mesquite, blue and foothill paloverde, ironwood, catclaw, and the exotic-looking elephant tree. There are many kinds of chollas and prickly pears as well as saguaro, organ pipe, senita, desert broom, ocotillo, sotol, desert agave, burro bush, and brittlebush. When the rains are right, vast expanses of the Lower Colorado Valley province are splashed with the multicolored hues of desert wildflowers and other ephemeral plants.

Other than on the Colorado River itself or along the Sonoyta River, the Lower Colorado Valley seems never to have supported permanent human settlements. The few Papagos who once lived here were hunting-gathering nomads. Insufficient rainfall prevented their farming; the few reliable sources of drinking water, including no more than a dozen springs and a few natural granite tanks holding the runoff from rare storms, required a small, dispersed, and highly mobile population if human beings were to survive. Moreover, creosote and bursage are not edible. Food plants are scarce; so is wildlife. Austerity in these commodities makes for a minimal size in the human population.

By contrast, the Arizona Upland vegetation province is a veritable cornucopia. It is a stem-succulent desert, with food-giving plants such as the foothill paloverde and prickly pears and chollas predominating in place of creosote and bursage. It is the heartland of the giant saguaro cactus; mesquite, ironwood, and acacias are larger and more abundant. There are barrel cactuses, beargrass, yuccas, and agaves. Organ pipe and senita are common in some areas—so are a host of annual plants with their vitamin-enriched leaves and protein-filled seeds. Pinyon, oak, and juniper grow in the higher elevations.

With this relative richness of plant life comes a fatter larder of animal life. Mountain sheep, mule deer, white-tailed deer and, in more recent times, peccaries, top the list of big game. Rabbits and other rodents are plentiful, as are lizards and other reptiles. Water, while still not abundant, is less a problem for human beings in this eastern two-thirds of the northern Sonoran Desert than in the western one-third. Permanent springs are numerous; there are rivers, such as the Santa Cruz, Magdalena, and Altar, which, though interrupted and intermittent, can be relied upon to supply year-round water at least in some stretches of their lengths; yearly rainfall is more assured. Papago life assumed its most anchored form along the rivers of the Arizona Upland country. Villages were largest here, and they were fixed. Hunting was good; gathering was even better. And reliable streams meant a better likelihood for crops of corn, squash, beans, chilis, and even cotton. Away from the rivers there were also villages, even as there are today. But in former times the pattern of life was one of back and forth movement between summer fields watered by annual rains and ephemeral drainageways and winter springs in the foothills above the valley floors. The floors were the beneficiaries of summer downpours, some of it in the form of direct rainfall but most of it dashing down mountain slopes in normally dry arroyos. In the desert, arroyos are great earthen conduits that deliver the life-giving power of water.

The foothill villages, situated near permanent springs, were the people's winter retreats. Thus there were summer homes and winter homes, a luxurious way to live even by modern standards.

Home for the Papago Indians, then, is a desert. It is not, however, some dry, scorched, monotonous land. It is a large world of endless contrasts, a home where the miracles of water are readily perceived. It is hot and cold; the summits of its peaks are opposed by the depths of its valleys. Coyotes, cactus wrens and other birds, wind whistling through saguaro spines, the beating whoosh of dust devils, summer storms, insects, croaking amphibians, the innocent rustling of some passing mammal or reptile—these would be alone in breaking the overwhelming silence were it not for man and his machines and domestic animals.

The cloudless sky is uniformly blue, although the depth and shades of blue change with the seasons. The western horizon is one of occasionally spectacular sunsets. The land is alternately rich and sparse in plant life. It is a setting in which cooperation fares better than competition; it can be relentless, but so can it be forgiving. Over

Harvesting cholla buds, Sycamore Canyon in Arizona

the long term, the Sonoran Desert is indifferent to man. But for men who would call it home, indifferent they cannot be. To remain a part of the desert requires knowledge, care, and not a little love.

Long ago, they say, when the earth was not yet finished, darkness lay upon the water and they rubbed each other. The sound they made was like the sound at the edges of a pond.

There, on the water, in the darkness, in the noise, and in a very strong wind, a child was born. One day he got up and found something stuck to him. It was algae. So he took some of the algae and from it made the termites. The termites gathered a lot of algae and First Born tried to decide how to make a seat so the wind could not blow it anywhere. This is the song he sang:

Earth Medicine Man finished the earth.
Come near and see it and do something to it.
He made it round.
Come near and see it and do something to it.

In this way, First Born finished the earth. Then he made all animal life and plant life.

There were neither sun nor moon then, and it was always dark. The living things didn't like the darkness, so they got together and told First Born to make something so the earth would have light. Then the people would be able to see each other and would live contentedly with each other.

So First Born said, "All right. You name what will come up in the sky to give you light."

They discussed it thoroughly and finally agreed that it would be named "sun."

Next First Born made the moon and stars, and the paths that they always follow. He said, "There will be plenty of prickly pears and the people will always be happy."

That's the way First Born prepared the earth for

us. Then he went away.

Then the sky came down and met the earth, and the first one to come forth was I'itoi, our Elder Brother.

The sky met the earth again, and Coyote came forth.

The sky met the earth again, and Buzzard came forth.

Elder Brother, Earth Magician, and Coyote began their work of creation, each creating things different from the other. Elder Brother created people out of clay and gave to them the "crimson evening," which is regarded by Papagos as one of the most beautiful sights in that region. The sunset light is reflected on the mountains with a peculiar radiance.

Elder Brother told the Papagos to remain where they were in that land which is the center of all things.

And there these Desert Indians have always lived. They are living there this very day. And from his home among the towering cliffs and crags of Baboquivari, the lonely, cloud-veiled mountain peak, their Elder Brother, I'itoi, spirit of goodness, who must dwell in the center of all things, watches over them.

John Schaefer drove the car; I sat next to him on the front seat. Danny Lopez, a Papago Indian, shared the back seat with all of our camera equipment. We rode over a well-traveled dirt road toward the village of Poso Verde (Green Well), or Ce:dagĭ Wahia as Papagos themselves say. Poso Verde, a desert oasis that takes its name from a permanent spring, is about a mile south of the international boundary just at the northern edge of the state of Sonora in Mexico. It is, therefore, a "Mexican" Papago village. I had been here once about twenty years previously. Danny had been here about ten years ago. It was John's first visit. It had taken us about an hour and a half to drive from Tucson west to Robles Junction, then south to the border crossing at Sasabe, Arizona. The pavement stopped in Arizona. In this part of Sonora, roads still belong to the desert. Blacktop awaits an uncertain future.

We drove south and west from Sasabe past a whole series of mesquite-fueled brick kilns. Making fired bricks out of adobe clay is perhaps the major industry among Mexicans in the Sasabe area, and the brick makers have erected two-story-high kilns that from a distance look like miniature Mayan temples.

Beyond the last of the kilns, and before we got to Poso Verde, we came to a small peak just west of the road, one I remembered from more than two decades earlier. It was the mountain, or *do'ag*, with two caves that were once the home of a wicked witch whom the Papagos called Ho'ok. We stopped the car, got out, and started the climb toward the caves. It was spring, and the brittlebush was in full yellow bloom. "That's Papago chewing gum," said Danny. "We call it *túhaws*." He explained that later in the year a resinous gum would be secreted on the lower stems, and that Papagos—especially the children—would pull it off the plant and chew it.

Ocotillo was also in bloom. Danny broke off a cluster of blossoms and rubbed them on his brown cheek. Where he rubbed the blossoms there were bright yellow streaks, a pollen cosmetic popular among women in times gone by. Then he pinched off the base of a single blossom and sucked the nectar from it, something all of us children did with honeysuckle where I grew up in northern California. Ocotillo, or *melhog*, is the Papagos' honeysuckle.

Up the mountain we clambered, a steep but short hike where there were no discernible trails, until we came to the ancient home of the witch, or Ho'ok *ki* (Ho'ok's house). Her "cave" was actually two caves side by side. One was very narrow, no more than five feet wide, and had a very high ceiling. The ceiling was in reality a fissure, a narrow cleft partially open to the sky and partially lodged with boulders that looked as if they might come tumbling down without too much provocation. From the mouth to the rear of the cave was no more than twenty feet.

Next to the fissure, with their floors at the same level,

was a low-ceilinged rock shelter, one perhaps fifteen feet wide and ten feet deep. A large broken metate, or stone grinding slab, lay on the surface of the midden that had accumulated over the centuries. Small human-like figures were painted on the overhanging stone in black and red. There were a few pieces of undecorated earthenware pottery lying around, even as there had been on the flat below the hill and on the slopes on our way up.

John scrambled back down to our car while Danny and I struggled our way the few extra feet above the caves to the summit of the hill. Here we found the remains of a small stone corral, and from here we had a magnificent view of the surrounding desert landscape. The houses of Poso Verde could be easily seen in the distance. Two or three huge turkey vultures, or buzzards, soared along on invisible air currents. We tried to walk to the top of the first cave to look down on the fissure, but the day was warming rapidly, and we felt we had to move along.

All of us returned to the car and drove into Poso Verde, stopping at the first house. A Papago couple was in the yard. The lady was shaping plant materials into wreath-like crosses to be hung outside the front doors of the houses in the village. Papagos, like neighboring Mexicans in the region, traditionally renew these crosses each year at the Fiesta de Santa Cruz (Feast of the Holy Cross). To have such a cross hanging near one's threshold protects the house and its occupants against lightning, which is an important consideration in a desert whose summers are wildly electric.

While Danny stayed to talk with this couple—both of whom were as fluent in English as Papago, and both of whom could probably speak Spanish as well—John and I walked to the spring that gives Poso Verde its name. This spring-fed reservoir, like other springs in the Sonoran Desert, is a miracle. There is no clue in the appearance of the surrounding cactus-studded volcanic hills to suggest an underground source of clear, cool, potable water. But there it is, and there it has been for nearly three hundred years of documented history. How much older than that?

A Holy Cross protects a storeroom against lightning, Ce:dagĭ Wahia (Poso Verde), Sonora.

No one is able to say with any certainty.

Poso Verde is a walk-in well. A trail descends to the water, now enclosed in a concrete-lined tank where one can scoop it into buckets or earthenware jars. Today there is a gasoline pump in the well so water can be forced conveniently into a pipe and delivered some distance away. The green or *verde* in the name comes not from the color of the water but from the color of the algae growing on rocks where the spring emerges from the earth. The algae has to be cleaned from the well periodically. On the day of our visit, the pool of water was clear, and there was little green color to be seen. Poso *verde* was poso *límpido*. Its life-giving substance flowed away from the well down a hand-dug canal to water a pasture and several fat and healthy-looking brown-and-white Hereford cattle. This liquid energy, in addition to supplying the domestic and gardening needs of the three families who lived here, also went toward keeping alive a small orchard of pomegranates and figs.

Danny, John, and I got back together at the house of Ascencio and Laura Antone. Ascencio, an elderly, wise, and worldly man—a fluent speaker of Papago and Spanish, but without much command of English—listened to Danny tell about our climb to Ho'ok's Cave. He asked if we would like to see the *ñe'ikud*, the "singing and dancing place" where Ho'ok was lured and put to sleep before being carried away to her death in the cave. Danny had thought the place was by a hill east of San Miguel, a place with stone walls and called locally "Ho'ok Muerta," or "Dead Witch" in a combination of Papago and Spanish. But it turned out that the people of Poso Verde have their own site for the event, and it was here, about a mile north of the village, that Ascencio guided us. Laura, his wife, came along.

We drove to the south side of a low pass through some hills lying immediately on the international boundary. In a fairly broad and level area there were the visible remains of what once had been a large stone corral, one about fifty-five by sixty-five yards. In the center of this big rectangle

Ascencio Antone makes a mesquite bowl,
Ce:dagĭ Wahia (Poso Verde), Sonora.

was a small circle of stones about six feet in diameter on the inside. An even smaller ring was annexed to the larger one on its south side. In the very middle of the larger ring a galvanized bucket was sunk into the ground. Its lid was a piece of cast iron; this was further weighted down by a very heavy blob of iron that had come from a stamp in an ore-crushing stamp mill. Except for an empty paper sack, the bucket was empty. Someone had left a few plastic flowers among some of the rocks; there were other mundane votive offerings to make it clear the site still functioned as a shrine. But Ascencio said that while ceremonies and dances were once held here, none had taken place in his lifetime. The stones remained *in situ*, but the desert had almost completely reclaimed with its prickly and shrubby growth what had once been a big cleared area.

According to Ascencio, the inner circle of rocks was where ceremonial paraphernalia for the dancing had been kept. The small annex was where ashes from ceremonial cigarettes had been carefully discarded. There had once been a house-like structure just beyond the corral of outer rocks where elders had met for important discussions. We saw the archaeological remains of this building.

I prevailed on Ascencio to tell the story of Ho'ok. He and Laura sat on the inner circle of rocks, and there, under the warm sun of late spring, he spoke with his voice and his hands. He paused occasionally to let Danny translate into English. We sat spellbound, as if enclosed by magic, listening:

Now the Papagos have a game of football in which the ball is not kicked but lifted and thrown a good ways by the foot, and Tash Siwani ("Sun Chief," or the sun) made such a ball out of red dust, and sent a young man to play it in the direction of the Salt River. And the young man did so.

Now be ready my poor brother,
And we will start to run.
Now before us our nice ball goes far.

Ascencio and Laura Antone tell the story
of Ho'ok, Ce:dagĭ Wahia (Poso Verde), Sonora.

26

After it we run.
No matter what kind of ground there is,
We must run over it.

As he kept the ball going on it came to the feet of a girl whose name was Woman-Who-Makes-Sleeping-Mats. She lived at a place called Hamṣ Va'aki (a prehistoric ruin). When she saw the ball which had rolled onto the mat she was weaving, she picked it up and hid it under the square of cloth which Indian girls wear.

And the young man came up and asked her if she had seen the ball, and she answered no, she had not seen it, and she kept on denying it, so at last he turned back and said he might as well go home as he no longer had a ball to play with. But he had not gone far before the girl called to him: "Are you not coming back to get your ball?" And he went back to her, and she tried to find the ball, but could not. So, after a time, the young man got angry and said, "All right, keep the red ball—but something terrible will happen to you because the red ball belongs to the Sun." Then he went away.

The woman was frightened. She tried to call the young man back. But she could not find the red ball. It had gone into her womb.

After the usual nine months, she gave birth to a baby girl, one with claws on its hands and feet like those of a wild animal. Every four days this baby girl grew very fast. In a short time she was as large as any of the children in the village.

And the people did not know what this meant, and they asked Coyote, and Coyote knew because this had been prophesied of old time. And Coyote said, "She is Ho'ok."

And Ho'ok grew and became able to crawl, but people were afraid of handling her because of the scratching of her claws. Only her relatives could safely handle her. They became afraid that she would harm their children, so some of the people went to a cave in the Baboquivari Mountains where I'itoi lived. They were surprised to see that I'itoi was like a tiny man, something like an old dwarf.

They told I'itoi the problem, and because Ho'ok claimed him as an uncle, he was able to talk to her. He found her at a little hill called Ho'ok Muerta, a place just east of San Miguel. He pointed to a mirage in the south, telling her it was her father. "You should go to your father," he told her.

So Ho'ok started toward the mirage, but she could never catch up with it no matter how far she went. When she got far to the south in Mexico, to a place called Crooked Ironwood Tree, she realized she could not reach her father. So she turned around and went back north until she came to a hill with a cave in it. She lived here like a wildcat, and in time became able to kill deer, antelope, and all big game. Yet, being part human, she would tan buckskin like a woman and do all that a woman needs to do.

The cave in the hill where she lived can still be seen. It is called Ho'ok's Cave.

Ho'ok acquired a taste for human flesh. When she heard a baby crying in the nearby village of Poso Verde, she would go to the house and offer to take the baby outside to comfort it. If the parents consented, she would take the baby outdoors, tear its intestines out, wrap the intestines around the house so the parents could not come out and interfere, and take the remains back to her cave, carrying them in her burden basket. There she would put the baby into a mortar, pound it up and eat it.

And the people called on I'itoi to help them, and I'itoi said, "I will kill her at once!"

And I'itoi, being her relative, went to her home and said, "Your grandchildren want some amusement and are going to have dances now every night and would like you to come." On three successive nights he asked her to come, but each time she refused. Finally, on the fourth night, she agreed.

Ho'ok got ready in the early evening and dressed herself in a skirt of soft buckskin. And over this she placed an overskirt of deerskin fringed with long cut fringes and deer hoofs at the ends to rattle. And then she ran to the Singing-and-Dancing Place; and the people could hear her a long way off, rattling, as she came. And they were already dancing when she arrived there, and she went and joined hands with I'itoi.

And Ho'ok was a great smoker, and I'itoi made a special cane cigarette that had something in it that would make folks sleep. He had prepared the cigarette by alternating a layer of real tobacco with a layer of the sleeping tobacco. He would smoke the real tobacco, hand the cigarette to her, and she would smoke the sleeping tobacco. Then he would take the cane back, smoke the layer of real tobacco, and so on.

The smoking and continual dancing made Ho'ok very sleepy. Several times she started to leave the dance to go to her cave, but every time the people stopped her. They knew she was frightened of rattlesnakes, so they hid in the bushes as she approached, rattling their rattles in imitation of the snake. This would make her run back to the dance area.

Finally, after four days and nights, she fell so soundly asleep that nothing could awaken her. So I'itoi carried her on his shoulder to her cave where people were already waiting with large stacks of firewood. He put her inside the cave and the people closed the entrance with a door they had made. They lighted a great bonfire, one that burned fiercely. When the fire reached Ho'ok she awakened and cried out: "My grandchildren, what have I done that you should treat me this way!"

And the fire hurt her so that she jumped up and down with pain, and her head struck the ceiling of the cave and split the rock. And when the people saw this they called to I'itoi, and he went up and put his foot over the crack, and sealed it up, and you may see the track of his foot there to this day.

We had not found I'itoi's footprint on our visit to the cave, although it is doubtless there somewhere. And could the broken metate we saw have been the "mortar" on which Ho'ok ground the bones of the children? About the cave where she was burned there can be no question. The walls are smoke blackened, and the fissure is still there where she struck her head on the ceiling.

Ascencio's admittedly abbreviated version of the story of Ho'ok, told most imperfectly here, ended. We looked again at our surroundings. Ho'ok, progeny of woman and the sun's kickball, devourer of Papago children, had been here before us. It was here that she had gone to sleep for the final time of her gruesome life. We went away pleased to have seen the site, but as products of western civilization, both John and I wondered: How old is it? When were these rocks put here? How long ago did the house fall into a mound?

Western man has his own witches. One of them has made it difficult for us to perceive reality unless numbers are attached: the height, width, and length of an object in feet or meters; the amount of something in weight, capacity, or cash value; the age of something in years. Such notions are irrelevant in the desert. They certainly meant nothing to Papagos in aboriginal times.

However, I remained bewitched. I was compelled to search my library to see what it might tell about the age of the places we had seen.

On February 12, 1699, Captain Juan Mateo Manje found himself in the company of Father Eusebio Kino, a Jesuit missionary, in the northern Sonoran Desert. Some 281 years before our most recent visit to Poso Verde, Manje and Kino had also been there. Manje wrote:

> On the 12th, after mass, we continued west over hills covered with pasture; and after five leagues, we came to a spring of crystal water which we named

Santa Eulalia. Nearby we found a small settlement [the village of Ce:dagĭ Wahia, or Poso Verde] where we counted 60 persons, who took us to a big square corral with stone walls. Near this there was a smoked cave on a rocky hill.

We were told that a giant monster with the features of a woman, mouth of a pig and claws of an eagle had come from the north and made his home in this cave. (I do not know whether they are telling a fable.) This monster would fly around catching as many Indians as he could to eat. The Pima [i.e., Papago] Indians began very carefully to gather large quantities of wood. One day the Indians invited the monster to this place and sacrificed for him two Indian prisoners they had caught from the enemies, with whom they were at war. When the monster was satiated, the Indians started a dance which lasted three days in the corral—built so that the monster would come in.

When the Indians who were dancing got tired and sleepy, others would take their place. When the monster became sleepy and went to his cave, the Indians followed him. When he was sound asleep, they closed the door of the cave with the wood they had gathered and set it on fire. The flames and smoke asphyxiated the monster, which died growling. Thus the Indians got rid of the terrible beast.

The places we had seen—the cave, the well, the village, and the stone corral—were those Manje and Kino had seen. The stories we heard from Danny and Ascencio were essentially those told to this officer in the army of Spain by anonymous Papagos in the late seventeenth century. The hill that was the home of Ho'ok; the spring that provided the people of Ce:dagĭ Wahia with their water; the stone corral; and all that one could see or imagine from the perspective of this place were—and still are—home to a whole people. The story of Ho'ok and dozens of other stories like it present the Papago claim to the desert.

The smoke-blackened cave with the fissure and the carefully built stone corral are seals of validation. And all this is taken for granted by the desert people. For them there need be no measurements in numbers of years; there are no international or regional and state boundaries. Like the cactuses and mesquite trees and like the red-tailed hawks and brown coyotes, they are perennial. It is the rest of us who are exotic and ephemeral.

"Into a Good Land"

"For the Lord thy God bringeth thee into a good land, a land of brooks of water, of fountains and depths that spring out of valleys and hills; a land of wheat and barley, and vines, and fig trees and pomegranates; a land of olive oil and honey; a land wherein thou shalt eat bread without scarceness. Thou shalt not lack anything in it, a land whose stones are iron and out of whose hills thou mayest dig copper."

Thus did Moses describe a desert, the Promised Land, to the Israelites.

"I am in a most fertile country," wrote Father Eusebio Kino. "There are already very rich and abundant fields, plantings and crops of wheat, maize, frijoles, chick-peas, beans, lentils, bastard chick-peas, etc. There are good gardens, and in them vineyards for wine for masses, with cane-brakes of sweet cane for syrup and *panocha*, and, with the favor of Heaven, before long for sugar. There are many Castilian fruit trees, such as fig trees, quinces, oranges, pomegranates, peaches, apricots, pear trees, apples, mulberries, pecans, prickly pears, etc., with all sorts of garden stuff, such as cabbages, melons, watermelons, white cabbage, lettuce, onions, leeks, garlic, anise, pepper, mustard, mint, Castilian roses, white lilies, etc., with very good timber for all kinds of building, such as pine, ash, cypress, walnut, china trees, mesquite, alders, poplar, willow, tamarind, etc.

"[There] are the plentiful ranches which are already stocked with cattle, sheep, and goats, many droves of mares, horses, sumpters — mules as well as horses — pack animals necessary for transportation and commerce, with very rich and abundant pastures all the year, to raise very fat sheep, producing much tallow, suet, and soap, which already is made in abundance.

"The climate of most of these lands...is very good and pleasant,...with neither too great heat nor too great cold.

"In these new nations and new lands there are many good veins and mineral lands bearing gold and silver; and in the neighborhood and even in sight of these new missions and new conversions some very good new mining camps of very rich silver ore are now being established."

The land of Canaan and the Sonoran Desert are half the world apart, but in the eyes of Moses and of Kino, they were the same: parched, semidesolate regions that could be turned to paradise through the grace of God and the labor of man. Their power of faith was stronger than their sense of reality.

Father Eusebio Kino, a priest in the Society of Jesus (Jesuits), was born in 1645 within the district of a tiny village a few miles northwest of Trent in the Tyrolian Alps within what is today a part of northern Italy. In 1681, prepared for his life's work as a missionary, he arrived in New Spain. Six years later, in 1687, he rode horseback headed northward over an unmarked boundary on the upper Río San Miguel in Sonora that separated the Opata and Eudeve Indians from the Pimans. The historian Herbert Bolton has called this boundary "the rim of Christendom," but it was more than that. The Opatas and Eudeves to the south had long been under missionary influence and under the influence of Spain generally. The Pimans of the northern Sonoran Desert, however, had neither missionary nor other European living among them until Kino's arrival. The "rim," therefore, was one that divided the highly structured, monarchical, expansionist state of Spain and the loosely organized, democratic, provincial, and isolationist communities of Piman Indians. South of the line was the New World of Europe; to its north was the very old world of the native inhabitants. Kino, determined to bring about "the conversion and salvation of the heathen Indians," became the bridge.

The "heathen Indians" whom Kino encountered in 1687 and among whom he expended his major efforts for the remaining twenty-four years of his life were one and the same only insofar as all of them spoke mutually intelligible dialects of the same language and all referred to themselves by a common term, O'odham. They shared the northern reaches of the Sonoran Desert, a few even living beyond the desert's pale to the east and southeast in the San Pedro and San Miguel river valleys. The southeasternmost village was Mututicachi, a settlement at the headwaters of the Río Sonora. The place was destroyed by Spanish soldiers in 1688 after its inhabitants were unjustly accused of having allied themselves with hostile tribes to the north and east. The Spaniards killed all the men and deported the women and children to the south.

The language spoken by the various groups of northern O'odham is related to the Uto-Aztecan family of languages, a family whose members include Nahuatl, the classic language of the Aztecs; the speech of Tarahumaras,

Yaquis, and Mayos; and the languages of the Cora, Huichol, Luiseño, and Cahuilla. The southernmost representative of Uto-Aztecan is Pipil, spoken as far south as northwestern Nicaragua; the northernmost Uto-Aztecan language is Northern Paiute (Paviotso) of southeastern Washington and southern Idaho.

Spaniards and other Europeans, including those who learned the native language, rarely referred to the O'odham by that name. Ignoring underlying linguistic, political, and social realities, they instead applied their own terms, labelling groups of Indians in ways that had little to do with the Indians' perceptions of themselves. It was thus that groups of southern O'odham speakers, including some who lived as far south as northern Jalisco, came to be lumped together under such tags as *Tepehuán*, *Tepecano*, *Névome Alto*, *Névome Bajo*, and *Pima Bajo*.

By 1645, Spain had pushed her people and her institutions northward along the western side of the Sierra Madre Occidental. As early as 1539 and 1540, Friar Marcos de Niza and the entire expedition of Francisco Vásquez de Coronado had passed through the region en route to New Mexico. Their impact on the northern O'odham, however, could only have been minimal. But in 1645, Franciscan missionaries came knocking at the door of the *Hímeris* (also Hymeres, Hymene, Himides, Hymeris, and Ímuris), described as "a very populous nation inhabiting the various valleys formed by the Sierra Madre, northwest of the Sonora Valley and extending to the inlet of California." These Indians, who clearly were northern O'odham, repulsed attempts of the Franciscans and their military escort to enter their country, and they remained free of direct foreign intervention for another forty-seven years. But in the meantime, in 1662, *Los Hímeris gentiles* (the unconverted Hímeris Indians) made its way onto a map, and for a while a name that the Indians probably applied to a single village, Imuris, became that for a whole group.

Sometime during the latter half of the seventeenth century, Spain's representatives discovered that the so-called *Hímeris* spoke dialects of a language surprisingly like that they had heard farther to the south. The designations *Névome Alto* and *Névome Bajo* had given way simply to *Pima Bajo* so it was logical that the northern speakers of O'odham should be called the *Pimas Altos,* or Upper Pimans, in contrast to the Lower Pimans. Similarly, the Pimería Baja, or land of the Lower Piman Indians, gave rise to the opposing Pimería Alta, land of the Upper Piman Indians.

Throughout his life, Father Kino's Sonora was the Pimería Alta. He, his contemporaries, and his eighteenth-century successors came to refer to the O'odham who lived there by a variety of names. Kino himself spoke of the "Sobas" who lived on the lower Río Altar, the Río Concepción, the Río Sonoyta, and the vast desert country surrounding those desert streams. His *Sobaipuris* (also Sobahipuris, Soba y Jipuris, and similar variations) were the natives of the San Pedro and parts of the Santa Cruz River valleys. The Pimas were the rest of the northern O'odham, but chiefly those who dwelled on the upper Magdalena, Cocospera, Magdalena, Gila, upper Altar, and upper and middle Santa Cruz rivers.

Other terms were used in the 1700s as well: *Piatos* (possibly an abbreviation for Pimas Altos); *Gileños* (for Gila River Pimas); and *Zimarrones* (Cimarrones, for the westernmost Pimans). Most important of all, because it is one of two labels for northern O'odham used by outsiders that has survived to the present time, was Papago.

Father Kino seems never to have used the word "Papago" in any of his writings; neither did he describe any part of the Pimería Alta as the Papaguería. The distinction of being the first person to do so seems to belong to Father Luis Velarde, Kino's successor, who in 1716 wrote a *Description of Pimería Alta.* In that description, written two years after his arrival in the region, he spoke of "the *Papabotas,* this is to say, Pima-bean-eaters, their principal harvest being beans called *javapi* ('*papabi*' in another source)."

Thus we have Father Velarde to thank for the folk etymology of the word "Papago," as "Papabote" (and similar variants) came to be consistently rendered by the mid-eighteenth century. His definition of Papagos as "bean eaters" or "bean people" has been followed by nearly everyone since his day. The term for tepary bean in O'odham is *bawi*. The plural is *ba:bawi*. This means "Pima bean people" would be *ba:bawi O'odham*, a possible—but highly improbable—source of "Papago."

Long before Father Velarde was born, in the 1560s and 1570s, cartographers Gerhardus Mercator and Abraham Ortelius drafted maps of America showing the eastern shores of the upper end of the Gulf of California—then called the Mar Vermeio ("Red Sea")—with a B[ahia, or Bay] del Papagaio. *Papagayo* is the Spanish word for "parrot" or "chatterbox." Is it a coincidence that the location on the map is in southwestern Papago Indian country? And coming from another direction, in Tarahumara country, east of the Papaguería, there is a settlement called Papigochic. The Jesuits Francisco María Pícolo and Juan María Salvatierra served in the Tarahumara in the late seventeenth century before serving terms in Sonora. Could one of them have brought the name "Papago" with him?

Regardless of the origin or meaning of the name, it is clear from eighteenth-century accounts that non-Indians used "Papago" to refer to Indians living in the riverless desert country south of the Río Gila, west of the Río Santa Cruz, north of the Río Concepción, and east of the Río Colorado. If the Pimas, Sobas, and Sobaipuris lived near the edges of the desert's streams, the Papagos, "naked and very poor," according to Captain Manje, lived on "sterile lands." Wrote Father Velarde: "The character of these Indians, especially of the north [i.e., Pimas and Sobaipuris], is haughty and proud, a fact which can be recognized in the manner in which they talk—with little esteem—about those Indians of the west [i.e., Papagos]. These western Indians, either because of being less haughty or because of some other motive, consider [Pimas and Sobaipuris] superior and look up to them with special respect."

By the end of the eighteenth century, the Sobaipuris, driven off by unrelenting attacks of Apache Indians, had abandoned the San Pedro River Valley in favor of the Gila and Santa Cruz. And also by the end of the eighteenth century, increasing numbers of O'odham, recruited by missionaries and attracted by better economic opportunities, had left their "sterile lands" to settle among the river-dwelling natives whose populations had shrunk in the face of lethal epidemics and Apache attack. "Sobaipuri" and "Soba" disappeared from the written records; only "Papago" and "Pima" survived.

Beneath the facile definitions of them by Spaniards there existed a quite different northern O'odham cultural reality. When Kino crossed the rim of Christendom on the upper Río San Miguel, the northern Pimans were involved in three different kinds of subsistence economies. Those who lived farthest west, from the head of the Gulf of California through the Pinacate Mountains and northward to the lower Gila River, appear to have been hunting-gathering nomads. Visited on more than one occasion in the late 1600s and early 1700s by Father Kino and Captain Manje, the latter described them as being "poor and hungry. . . . little given to work. They live on the roots and wild fruits which the region produces at various times of the year. They also eat shellfish, worms, lizards, iguanas, and other animals considered repugnant by us, and with bow and arrow hunt for wild sheep [and deer]. The men go about naked, and the women are scantily clothed in a few tatters of antelope skin [or small pieces of hare furs] extending from waist to mid-calf. . . . At certain seasons of the year they live on fish [from the Gulf of California]."

There is no mention of crops; nor does he mention houses and other native architecture. The historical picture drawn of these western O'odham is precisely what one would expect for a people subsisting in one of the hottest and driest environments in North America. By migrating seasonally to take advantage of the movement of game, including fish swimming in and out of the head of the Gulf of California, and of the annual leafing, fruiting, and seeding of edible desert plants, it was possible for a small number of people to eke out a bare existence.

They were unencumbered by material possessions save a few vessels of earthenware pottery. Their settlements were seasonal camping sites located either near ephemeral springs or natural stone tanks in the mountains that store water from infrequent summer cloudbursts or minimal winter rains.

How many such Pimans there were, how many groups of them, and precisely how they may have been related to one another is now impossible to say. A figure of 250 to 300 people living off this vast expanse of land in the northwestern Sonoran Desert is probably generous. Today, there is no one here who depends on the region's native products for food and clothing. The few inhabitants are here by dint of western technology. And there are no longer any Papagos among them except for a very few who work on shrimp boats at Puerto Peñasco on the upper Gulf of California. In the United States, the Cabeza Prieta Game Range and Luke Air Force Range are totally uninhabited.

To the east of the hunting-gathering nomads and south, west, and north of river-dwelling Pimans were people referred to by Father Jacobo Sedelmayr in 1746 as members of "the Pima-Papago tribes . . . [who] live in a dry and sterile desert which is difficult to reach." In 1744 an anonymous Spaniard wrote of these Papagos that they "live during the summer on the plains [i.e., in the valleys], making watering holes or wells from which to drink, where during the rainy season are sown corn, beans, and squash—and very little of these. As soon as the crops are consumed, the [Papagos] spread out among the rancherías or pueblos of the other Pimas to serve them as laborers, but only for the purpose of getting food."

Although none of the known eighteenth- and early nineteenth-century accounts makes mention of the fact, it appears safe to assume that a pattern of living characteristic of Papagos in the late nineteenth century prevailed then—and prehistorically—as well. The region is one where there are no permanent streams and where the only reliable sources of year-round water are small springs located in the foothills of mountains where farming would be difficult to impossible. The result, according to anthropologist Ruth Underhill, was that:

> . . . a village was not a constant unit, for desert conditions, before the digging of government wells, did not permit of year-long residence in any one place. In the summer when rains filled the shallow reservoirs scooped out with blades of wood and stone, the people could live in the flat country whose name is the same as that for "land" and "ground" and here they could have their fields near the mouths of washes [aki ciñ]. Such a farming settlement was not known as a village but as Fields [oidag], since these were the important thing.
>
> The fields could be occupied only during the summer rainy season and as long afterward as the water lasted in the reservoir: then the people must move to the foothills where there were springs. Each Field had its foothill camp, known as the Well [wahia], where its residents kept duplicates of the objects they could not transport, such as metates and water jars, and where they had at least the posts for a shelter. Sometimes one Well would not accommodate all the Field people and then they had several. Sometimes two related villages used the same Well, but then they kept apart. . . . When one changed his Field village, for good reason, he was still not expected to change his Well village. Relationships in each were permanent.
>
> The result was that each village had a dual existence, in summer at the Fields, and in winter at the Wells. Many censuses have come to grief over this difficulty. But Field and Well together were part of a larger group. In the course of time, the villages had proliferated, sending out one group after another to look for more land. The new settlement thus made might be only a suburb of the home village, obeying its officials and coming home for ceremonies. But sometimes the daughter village was so large

Juanita Ahil cooks saguaro fruit at a saguaro-harvest camp in the Tucson Mountains in Arizona.

or so far away that it needed a leader of its own. Then it appointed one, but considered him always a subsidiary to the leader of the parent village.... On great ceremonial occasions, all daughter villages returned in a body to the parent village. If intervillage games were held, it was understood that all played or bet on the same side. If one went on the warpath, the others were notified and asked to join.

... Some Papago made a business of trading trips to the Pima, to Mexico and to the Yuma. These were a winter occupation on the same basis as hunting and sometimes combined with it. The Papago were homeless in the winter and many of them, instead of camping at the Well village, wandered about trading their goods or their labor for enough to support them until the wet season came again.

Thus the Papagos of the central Pimería Alta were two-village people in the sense that they had summer houses by their fields in the valleys and winter houses by the springs or wells in the nearby foothills. They were able to raise perhaps a fifth of the food they ate by practicing what has variously been called flash-flood, *ak chin* (arroyo mouth), or *de temporal* (rainy weather) farming. At the mouths of arroyos people built brush dams to spread water from summer thunderstorms over adjacent fields. Corn, beans, and squash were planted as soon as the fields were wet, usually in July or August. With luck, there was a harvest in October or November.

Deer, mountain sheep, mountain lions, doves, rabbits, and other rodents were Papago game. The fruits, seeds, roots, stems, and leaves of many dozens of desert plants were collected and consumed in season, with the fruit of the saguaro or giant cactus heading the list. The blackening of seeds in saguaro fruit, marking its ripeness, signalled the Papago new year, normally in late June. It has been estimated that as recently as the 1920s and 1930s Papagos harvested about 450,000 pounds of saguaro fruit annually. Some was eaten fresh; some was dried and shaped into

The kitchen in a saguaro-harvest camp
in the Tucson Mountains in Arizona

cakes; some was dried, ground, and converted into meal. There were also saguaro syrup and saguaro jam. Most fruit, however, was ultimately consumed in the form of a fermented drink called *nawait*, saguaro wine. The only native alcoholic beverage among Papagos, with the possible exception of a beer brewed from mesquite beans, *nawait* was prepared and drunk at a yearly three- or four-day ceremony designed to "bring down the clouds." Without summer rains there would be no crops. Neither would there be any life in the desert.

What the two-village Papagos failed to grow, hunt, or gather they were able to get by trading with river-dwelling Pimans, giving their labor or such items as baskets, wild products, deer hides, and salt in exchange for agricultural products. When Spanish and Mexican settlements sprang up near Papago country, the same trading relationships were extended to them.

The third kind of subsistence economy belonging to the Pimería Alta was that made possible by the region's more-or-less permanent, albeit interrupted, streams. O'odham who lived along the rivers, including the Gila, Santa Cruz, San Pedro, San Miguel, Magdalena, Altar, Concepción, and Sonoyta, were those whom Father Velarde said were "haughty and proud." Water, the desert's great centripetal force, draws to itself the richest abundance of living matter. It is along streams that plants can be most easily gathered, game most conveniently hunted, and crops most readily and assuredly grown.

It has been asserted that in pre-Kino times, or before the 1680s, there were Piman Indians in northern Sonora who practiced irrigation agriculture. In virtually every instance in which Spaniards write of Piman fields with canals, however, Spanish-introduced wheat or other exotic crops are also mentioned as being grown. It would appear more likely that canal irrigation was introduced—or reintroduced, since it had been practiced in the northern Sonoran Desert until sometime in the 1400s—by Spaniards. Irrigation seems not to have been a northern Piman prehistoric custom. Instead, the river-dwelling natives apparently took advantage of the rivers' flood plains, planting their corn, squash, and beans in fields watered by the rivers' summer rainstorm overflow. They also grew cotton from which they wove cloth on horizontal looms for blankets and clothing.

The Piman settlements along the rivers were numerous and large. Father Kino's mother mission of Dolores had more than a hundred natives in 1687; there were "more than five hundred souls" at Tubutama and more than seven hundred at Saric early in 1691; there were more than forty houses "close together" at Tumacacori in 1691; and on his first visit to San Xavier del Bac in 1692, Kino noted it contained more than eight hundred people. He visited San Marcelo del Sonoydag (i.e., Sonoyta, Sonora) in October 1700, and wrote that "it has very near here more than a thousand souls." Granting Kino's possible tendency to exaggerate population size, it is nonetheless clear that by far the largest Pimería Alta settlements were —and still are—along its streams.

Although the riverine Pimans had fields that were removed some distance from their permanent dwellings, most of them seem to have been essentially one-village dwellers. Rivers supplied year-round drinking water as well as water for summer crops. There was no need to migrate from summer village to winter village but only to walk from one's permanent place of residence to one's fields on a sporadic basis in season. There were no doubt shelters built next to the fields where people could camp for varying periods of time, giving them the appearance of "villages" when they were occupied. And some Pimans, such as the Kohadks, may have taken advantage of both riverine and *ak chin* farming opportunities, moving from the Gila River south to a place in the desert where flash-flood farming could be practiced.

Whether living in the desert or next to desert rivers, Pimans were organized on the basis of parent and daughter villages as described by Ruth Underhill. Additionally, however, they were divided into dialect groups. The members of a dialect group, besides sharing distinctive patterns of speech, also shared historical and other traditions that set them apart from one another. The dialect group was the Piman version of "us guys" as opposed to "you guys," with its members regarding themselves as *the* O'odham. If Spaniards were aware of the presence of such units beyond their conceptualizations of Pimas, Sobaipuris, Sobas, and Papagos, the written record fails to show it.

Modern observers have counted as many as nine Papago dialect groups. Linguists Dean and Lucille Saxton have listed the *Huhhu'ula* (possibly meaning grandmother's children, i.e., orphans); *Gigimai* (braggarts); *Huhuwosh* (or Huhumu, meaning unknown); *Ko-lohdi* (or Kok-lolodi, from the Spanish word *tecolote*, owl); *Ge Aji* (big narrow place); *Ahngam* (having desert willows); *Kohadk* (dried and burned); *Totoguani* (loose G-string, or possibly a term describing the guttural cast of the speech of the people); and the *Hiach-eD O'odham* (Sand Papagos) or the *S-ohbmakam*. The latter, possibly the Soba of the Spaniards, is especially interesting. The root may be either *ohbgam*, the Papago word for a species of paloverde, or *ohb*, enemy (usually an Apache), making the *S-ohbmakam* the "Paloverde People" or "Enemy People." The Saxtons consider *Hiach-eD O'odham* and *S-ohbmakam* different terms for the same dialect group when, in fact, they may be different groups.

There were probably more such dialect units in times past, their members long since having been integrated with other Papagos, thereby losing their distinctive identities. This is surely the case with the Sobaipuris, two segments of whom are known to have lived in the San Pedro River Valley and one known to have been the earliest O'odham inhabitants of San Xavier del Bac. Some living Papagos speak of the original residents of San Xavier del Bac as the *Wakon O'odham*, or "Baptized People," a clear reference to their early conversion to Christianity.

The political organization of the natives of Pimería Alta was as effective as it was simple. There was no single large "tribe" in the sense of a hierarchical structure of all the region's O'odham people under central leadership. The "tribes" are more likely to have been the dialect groups made up in turn of groups of related villages. The headman or "chief" of such a tribe held office because of his personal traits of character rather than through inheritance. He might have been a Wise Speaker (ritual orator); a Keeper of the Smoke (the organizer and principal speaker at community meetings); Keeper of the Medicine Basket (in charge of the group's sacred paraphernalia); or The One Above (a person with "great man" social status). He was assisted in his duties by men who were Legs (runners), Eyes (lookouts), or Voices (village criers). Different men might lead on other occasions. There were leaders for war, games, the hunt, and songs.

Except that women did not take part in council meetings, the system was democratic in the extreme. The headman's authority rested on group consensus. All adult males had to agree before a decision could be made that affected the entire community or group. And all adult males were considerably influenced by their wives.

Settlements, excluding the western nomads, were laid out in a similar fashion. Private structures were arranged in family compounds. They included dome-shaped brush houses, storage units, a cooking enclosure, and a shade or *ramada* that was simply a flat roof supported on poles. Compounds were widely scattered in a *ranchería*-style settlement pattern. The single public structure was a large circular brush building with a comparatively flat roof. Council meetings were held here, and the annual fermenting of saguaro wine took place here as well. Because the headman was responsible for the upkeep of this round house, it was located near his compound. And because the village crier sat on the roof of the round house to shout announcements to the entire village, it had to be located within shouting distance of all the family compounds.

O'odham architecture shared a single characteristic: it was dry. No water was required in northern Piman construction. Houses, enclosures, storage units, and public or ceremonial structures were made entirely out of materials from cactuses, trees, shrubs, grasses, or other plants.

Ramadas and round houses had mud roofs only when rain fell on dirt that had been thrown there. Such architecture indicates the unwillingness of Pimans, even those who lived along streams, to "waste" the desert's most precious asset, its water. Furthermore, it gave their lifestyle the tenor of a people who were camping out rather than settled in. They lived very lightly on the land, ready to move at a moment's notice. Mobility was one of the keys to their success. Pimans' dry construction, moreover, stood in sharp contrast to the monumental mud construction of some of their prehistoric predecessors in the region, earlier peoples who mistakenly believed they had come to the desert to stay.

"Poor as the Papago country was," writes Ruth Underhill, "its economics were those of abundance. Papagos did not hoard property; . . . they were constantly giving, as though from an inexhaustible supply. The answer is that the supply, meagre though it was from the modern point of view, was sufficient, for their simple needs and more."

She continues:

> Food was the principal gift and food will not keep in that hot country except in dehydrated form. Because of the migratory life, it must be left unguarded in storehouses and caches, subject to attack by animals or enemies. Better to dispose of any surplus while it was available and palatable and thus invest in good will! And anything but starvation rations was considered a surplus. The standard meal was corn meal gruel: luxuries much beyond that were donated with lavish hand and never missed.
>
> Giving became the regular Papago investment. . . . One who gained the reputation for stinginess had damned his prospects in village and family life while the lavish giver not only achieved honor but had a continual income pouring in. For all gifts were returned, in equal quantity and more. The constant exchange of goods in the form of gifts was the Papago equivalent for trade. . . . Papago economics

involves principally the study of groups which had gift relations.

The center of the system was the patriarchal family which, rather than the individual, must be taken as the unit both of property holding and of gift exchange. The family was a business concern, producing and disposing of goods under the direction of its male and female heads, and such production meant a full time occupation. This was not the sort of society where the men, when not hunting or fighting, had the privilege of leisure: the men were day laborers like the women. All rose with the morning star, rested in the heat of noon and did not stop work until dark. It was slow motion labor, for the heat forbids haste. But is was unremitting. Industry was the prime virtue. . . .

In short, Piman survival depended on cooperation rather than on competition. In the face of obvious scarcity, one behaved as if there were abundance. Through gifts, ceremonial exchanges, and gambling the people spread what available wealth there was fairly evenly throughout the entire group. Human beings invested in one another rather than in material goods. To do otherwise was to invite isolation, and there is no place in the desert for islands.

Taken in total, Pimans believed in and practiced something they continue to refer to as *O'odham himdag*. In a very narrow sense, this is Piman Indian religion. But in a much truer sense, it was the Piman "way," as in "way of life." *O'odham himdag* ultimately involved all things, all people, and all actions. It concerned the rights, dignity, and propriety—as well as the potential power— of human beings, of ceremonies, of living things, and of such life-giving entities as salt, the sun, and the ocean (from whence rains come). As Daniel Matson and I have written elsewhere:

The Piman Way was reinforced among its followers by the threat of the diseases which could befall one who transgressed against it—the principal role of the shaman [or medicine man] being to diagnose and direct cures for such illnesses. It was further supported by a rich ceremonial life, with ceremonies involving growth of crops, hunting, warfare, community health, and, above all, the bringing down of life-sustaining rain.

When Father Kino, his contemporaries, and his successors encountered the people of Pimería Alta, they came upon men, women, and children who were the bearers of an ancient and eminently successful desert culture. The O'odham had evolved their own religious beliefs. They had their own political, social, and economic structures. They spoke a complex language; they possessed a technology and a material culture, including architecture, ideally suited to their immediate surroundings. And finally, until Europeans came, they were altogether self-sufficient, depending on one another and on their desert environment to sustain them in their enjoyment of life. The Lord, their God—or Someone—had long ago brought them into a good land.

Canned Peaches

The old man was standing there in the Covered Wells trading post. He was using a spoon to eat peaches out of a can. The new priest had been told in advance by his fellow Franciscan, a missionary of long experience, that the old man had no use for white men. It was rumored he could speak English but chose never to do so.

The young friar, anxious to try out the Papago he had been studying since his arrival on the reservation, walked over to the venerable elder and said, "I hear you don't like the white man, that you won't speak English, and that you don't want anything to do with us. But here you are eating our peaches!"

Refusing to answer the priest directly, he said something to a younger Papago standing next to him. The younger man translated the response: "He says he hates the white man, but he likes their canned peaches."

And in the nearly three hundred years since Father Kino brought peaches with him to the Pimería Alta, that has been one of the major dilemmas of Papagos. How does one accept what are perceived to be the many blessings of an alien society and at the same time maintain a sense of independence, dignity, and self-esteem? The products of western civilization have strings attached; there is, to borrow a cynical expression, no free lunch.

Not that the bestowal of foreign blessings has always met with open-armed acceptance on the part of the O'odham. The people of Remedios told Kino in 1687 that they "neither wished to be Christians nor to have a missionary father." And one of the reasons they gave was that missionaries "pastured so many cattle that the watering places were drying up." One would think that the Pimans, who had no cattle or horses, would be delighted to have a gift of them. Deer, mountain lions, antelope, and mountain sheep had to be hunted; the sole aboriginal means of transportation was on foot. Cattle, on the other hand, could be raised and slaughtered at will, and horses provided an easy way to get around. The people of Remedios, though, had had ample opportunity to see the effects of cattle on desert watering places among the neighboring missionized Eudeve and Opata Indians to the south. Water took O'odham priority over meat and horseback riding.

Kino noted, however, that "gradually things were remedied and...the natives of this Pimería became so inclined to our holy faith that from places farther inland...they asked for fathers and holy baptism." They also received, whether asked for or not, a full eighteenth-century inventory of European plants and domestic animals that could be raised successfully in the Sonoran Desert. Winter wheat expanded the potential for farming among riverine dwellers; livestock marked the beginnings of pastoralism among people who formerly had relied on hunting, gathering, and small-scale farming for their subsistence.

Two hundred and one years after Kino's death, the process of the foreign bestowal of blessings on Papagos continued in much the same way. An entry on a Papago calendar stick, a kind of mnemonic device that enabled its keeper to recall a record of annual events in the history of Papagos, tells the story:

1912: The village of Santa Rosa, like all the other agricultural villages, is situated a long way from permanent water. During seasonable times water could be had from the wash, but when the wash was dry water had to be carried from a spring in a small range of mountains almost eight miles away. One old man said that before horses were introduced, the women went early in the morning with ollas and returned by the hottest time of the day.

This year the Government service decided to drill a well in the village, charging the cost to tribal funds. The chief objected to the move. He called his advisors into consultation and laid the matter before them. After a long discussion, it was unanimously decided to reject the offer. "For," they said, "although we do not have to pay for the well now, sooner or later the money must come. The People have lived a long time on their lands and prospered without this improvement and they wish to continue to live without the gratuitous assistance of anyone."

Nevertheless, later a white man came and took the chief with him to a certain spot where there was an ant hill, stuck a stick into the ground and said, "Here a well shall be drilled." It was done.

When the well was finished the chief told his people that the well must be left alone and, in order that the Papagos might continue their old life, water must still be carried from the spring in the foothills. Gradually, however, and very reluctantly, for the

Papagos are usually obedient to their chiefs, they began to disobey and get water from the well. The chief vainly threatened them and used all his power of persuasion to stop them. Matters continued in this unsatisfactory condition until one night the water supply in the house of the chief became exhausted and he was taken with thirst. He slipped out to the well to replenish his olla. Several of the tribesmen caught him in the act and charged him with inconsistency. The matter was settled by an agreement that all should use the water from the well.

To know about the history of relationships between Papagos and non-Indians is to know about the use of carrot and stick. Members of societies organized as states, specifically those of Spain, Mexico, and the United States, have in succession tried to transform members of the Papagos' traditionally stateless society into beings who resemble the would-be transformers. For three centuries Papagos have been encouraged directly, the stick, and indirectly, the carrot, to become Spaniards, Mexicans, and Anglo-Americans. The results to date have been very uneven; the process continues and perhaps always will. What is remarkable is that there remain a people, the "Papagos," whose constituents go right on thinking and behaving in ways that are uniquely their own. They still view themselves as Papagos; they show no signs of disappearing as a distinctive cultural entity.

The missionary program directed at Papagos throughout the eighteenth century was systematically designed to bring about their total conversion, not only from "paganism" to Christianity but also from being Indians to becoming loyal, tax-paying citizens of the Spanish Crown. By Spanish rule and law, the process was to be completed in no more than ten years. It was the job of the missionaries, with help from the military if necessary, to effect Indian assimilation. This was to be accomplished in four stages.

Stage one was the mission (*misión*) stage, during

which initial contacts were made with the natives and discussions were opened on the subject of God and the King, with royal vassalage being nearly as important as eternal salvation. In this beginning phase, the emphasis was on preaching and on winning the confidence of hoped-for converts.

Stage two involved either a reduction (*reducción*) or a conversion (*conversión*). A reduction entailed reducing the territory of the Indians by bringing them in "out of the wilderness" to a segregated community centered around a church and under the strict guidance of missionaries. This could be accomplished by persuasion or by force. A conversion, on the other hand, simply involved building a church in an already existing native population center, staffing it with missionaries, and preventing anyone other than Indians, clerics, and a possible small contingent of soldiers from living there. In the case of Pimería Alta, all of the mission centers became conversions rather than reductions. Never were troops sent out to round up Papagos to force them to live in a settlement not of their own choosing. And Papagos who moved from the desert to riverine conversions seem to have done so without much persuasion. Once there, moreover, they seem to have come and gone at will.

The third stage was called a doctrine (*doctrina*). By this time the Indians were to have been baptized and converted to Christianity, but they were still in need of instruction on the finer points of the new faith. The priest responsible for such teaching, a *doctrinero,* could be either a missionary father who was a member of a regular religious order with its own head and hierarchy or a secular priest who "lived in the world" and answered directly to a bishop.

The fourth and final stage in the assimilation process involved the curacy (*curato*), what one would consider today simply to be a parish church under the leadership of secular clergy. So long as Indians were in the charge of missionaries, the royal treasury was responsible for paying the bills, including salaries of priests, and Indians were tax exempt. When the missionaries left, however, secular clergy took over, and Indians were regarded as tax-paying citizens of Spain and were subjected to the same obligations and rights as those of any other citizen.

In the case of Papagos, the final two stages are largely only of academic interest. Throughout the eighteenth century, Papagos remained involved solely with regular clergy, first with the Jesuits (1687–1767) and finally with the Franciscans (1768–1843). Their mission communities —in spite of ten-year plans—never moved beyond the stage of conversions. When the secularization of former O'odham missions got under way in the 1840s during the early years of the Republic of Mexico, most of them had been all but abandoned by Pimans and taken over by *gente de razon*, non-Indian Mexicans whose native language was Spanish and who regarded themselves as the "people of reason." Other former mission communities, chiefly because of Apache attacks, had been abandoned by everyone. Guevavi was deserted by 1775; Santa Ana del Quiburi had been given up in 1762. The people of Tumacacori moved *in toto* to the comparative safety of San Xavier del Bac in 1848, and Cocospera gave up the ghost soon after 1864. Its Piman population had long since departed.

Of all the conversions founded by Father Kino, only one, San Xavier del Bac in Arizona, remains in Indian hands. It is still a major Papago settlement; the church serves a Papago parish. A few Papagos continue to live in Caborca, Sonora, but they are a tiny minority in a very large Mexican city. Their one-time mission church, built by Franciscans in the first decade of the nineteenth century, is now used only on special occasions. Otherwise, it belongs chiefly to dozens of roosting pigeons.

Mission communities aside, the impact of Spain in the Pimería Alta between the arrival of Kino in 1687 and the formation of an independent Mexico in 1821 was a major and lasting one. Christianity in the form of Roman Catholicism, with its full panoply of saints, heros and heroines, ritual, music, and religious art, came and stayed. So did a new architecture, one requiring water to shape mud bricks out of adobe clay and one entailing buildings

*Main altar in the abandoned church of St. Margaret Mary,
Emika, Arizona*

with square or rectangular floor plans and straight-sided walls with windows. Although Papagos never responded favorably to the plan, and they abandoned it when left to their own devices, there was a new settlement pattern that called for dwellings built in rows around a square or plaza on three sides with a church on the fourth. Papagos preferred the privacy of more-or-less randomly scattered family compounds. The European notion of private ownership of real estate and its attendant geometric grid plan for towns and cities was beyond the pale of Papago experience and understanding.

Many Papagos learned Spanish as a second language, and their own language was enriched by the infusion of Papago-pronounced Spanish words for new items in the cultural inventory. For example, the Spanish horse, *caballo*, became the Papago *kawyu*, and the Spanish saddle, *silla*, became the Papago *si:l*. The complete list is an extensive one.

Spanish livestock and farming technologies became a part of the Papago way of life. Plows were introduced, and these were pulled by horses, oxen, or mules. Floodplain farming came to be augmented or replaced by irrigation agriculture. Metal tools such as metal-bladed shovels, hoes, picks, and axes grew rapidly in demand after their initial appearance among Papagos. Among other things, picks and shovels made it possible to dig wells for water, thus tapping hidden underground supplies.

By sometime in the nineteenth century, most Papagos had adopted European-style clothing, covering the upper and lower parts of their bodies with shirts, skirts, blouses, and trousers in conformity with others' conceptions of modesty. European ornaments, such as glass beads, had become Papago jewelry as well. And by the nineteenth century, many Papagos had doubtless learned to play Spanish-introduced fiddles and guitars, to dance Spanish-style dances, and to sing popular Spanish songs of the day.

Spaniards, beginning in Father Kino's time, also instituted Spanish political offices in Piman communities. Staffs or canes of office were distributed to natives appointed by Spaniards to serve as governors, captains, *alcaldes* (civil officials with judicial, legislative, and executive functions), *topiles* (policemen), *fiscales mayores* (head church officers), *alguaciles* (sheriffs), and *fiscales ordinarios* (minor church officials). There was also the *temastián* who was taught the Spanish words for the catechism as promptly as possible and who subsequently served as catechist and also as a translator for the priest.

This system of political and religious functionaries, which carried the weight of Spanish authority, was superimposed on the Papagos' form of government. In some instances the native Keeper of the Smoke or traditional headman may also have been appointed governor; in others, no doubt, Spanish appointments ignored native leaders and leadership roles. Either way, some of these Spanish-introduced status positions, especially that of governor (*gobernador* in Spanish and *kownal* in Papago), survived well into the 1930s when Anglo-Americans imposed still another form of government. Indeed, even today the putative leader of all the Papagos who continue to live in Sonora is officially referred to as the "governor general." And at San Xavier del Bac, the leader of the twelve-man committee in charge of putting on the important village feasts throughout the year in observance of certain saints' days and other religious holidays has as his badge of office a silver-headed cane. His assistants wear ribboned medals.

More important than political positions as such was the Spaniards' conception of Piman "tribal" or governmental units and the degree to which Pimans ultimately accepted these definitions as their own. There is no way to know precisely when diverse groups of O'odham began 'to react to such oversimplified concepts as "Pima" or "Papago" or to understand that they were being lumped together for the administrative convenience of conquerors. The power to define is absolute power, and this important process that began in Spanish times has by no means reached a conclusion. Many people still feel a stronger loyalty to their immediate and extended families, to their villages, and to others in their dialect group than to an abstract invention of foreigners, one called "Papago."

Relations between most Papagos and Spaniards and Mexicans were relatively peaceful, especially when compared to the histories of such groups as Yaquis, Seris, Tarahumaras, and Apaches. Even the "peaceful Pueblos" of New Mexico staged a successful revolt against Spanish domination in 1680, an uprising that kept their country free of foreign intruders for twelve years. Three times before the middle of the nineteenth century, however, there were major episodes of armed conflict between O'odham and the "people of reason." And as recently as 1898, there was a shooting scrape between Papagos and Mexicans in the border town of El Plomo in Sonora.

The first Piman "rebellion" took place in 1695, a mere eight years after Father Kino's arrival. As historian Charles Polzer has said, "It was not a revolution, but rather a violent resistance to changes imposed by strange and powerful invaders." The immediate place of conflict was at Tubutama. The Jesuit priest at the mission, Father Janusque, said his Indians were discontented, that two of them were haranguing the rest, and that his life was in danger. Spanish troops were dispatched to the scene, and the "heads and disturbers" were punished "in sight of the rest," either by hanging or flogging. Moreover, an Opata Indian servant in the employ of the priest had, according to Father Kino, been "very harsh and had dealt maliciously with the Pimas, often beating them severely."

These and other resentments came to a head on March 29, 1695. Tubutama's Pimans killed the "harsh and malicious" Opata and two other Opatas besides. On April 2, in the company of more Pimans from mission settlements downriver from Tubutama on the Río Altar, the men who had risen in revolt went to Caborca where they martyred Father Francisco Saeta, the recently arrived missionary. They also killed Saeta's Indian helpers from outside the region: a Pima from Ures and men from elsewhere in Sonora. Before it was over, eight people were killed by the Tubutamans and their neighbors.

During the feverish aftermath there was a "peace" parley that resulted in the massacre of forty-eight Pimans. In the estimation of Father Kino, only eighteen of them had been involved in the revolt; the other thirty were totally innocent of any wrongdoing. This wanton slaughter on the part of the Spanish military led to further Piman rampages throughout the countryside. All the buildings were burned at Tubutama and Caborca; it was the same at Imuris, San Ignacio, and Magdalena. By September, the Spaniards succeeded in making a show of military force, Father Kino exerted his extraordinary influence as a man of peace, and the first Piman uprising came to an end. The missionization program moved ahead.

The second Piman revolt took place in 1751. The immediate scene of trouble was again the upper Río Altar, this time at the village of Saric a few miles north of Tubutama. A native of Saric, Luís Oacpicagigua, had been appointed captain general of all the Pimas by Sonoran Governor Diego Ortiz Parilla. Angered because of personal insults made against him by missionaries and other Spaniards and possibly anxious to affirm his position as a headman among his own people, he started a revolt by killing eighteen Spaniards he had invited to his house. Matters quickly spread from there. Father Enrique Ruhen was martyred at Sonoyta and Father Tomás Tello at Caborca. Before it was all over, Luís and his allies managed to kill more than a hundred of their enemies, and most mission stations were temporarily abandoned. Spanish soldiers killed more than forty Pimas, and in March 1752, Luís surrendered. He was subsequently taken prisoner and died in jail about 1754. One of the immediate results of the 1751–52 rebellion was the establishment of Spanish *presidios*, or forts, at Tubac and Altar.

An increased Spanish military presence in the Pimería Alta and the death of Luís by no means brought an end to armed hostilities. In 1756 a group of Papagos sacked San Xavier del Bac, and throughout the remainder of the eighteenth century, other groups of Piman apostates as well as pagans appeared in the records as enemies of the Spaniards. They were usually allied with Seris, Apaches, or other disaffected natives of northwestern Mexico. This provided further proof, if any was needed, that there was no Pima or Papago "nation," but rather a collection of little nations whose people had concerns that were more local than regional. Never were all the O'odham of the Pimería Alta allied under a single leader, nor were they ever bound together in a single cause.

One of the most dramatic records—almost melodramatic—left to us of an eighteenth-century battle with Piman Indians is in a letter written by Father Pedro Font. Father Font was a Franciscan missionary at Magdalena in November 1776, when the mission and village were attacked. The Indians living there were all Pimans; so were some of the attackers. A portion of Father Font's letter, written to the Father Guardian of the Apostolic College of Holy Cross of Querétaro, tells what happened:

The 16th day [of November 1776] dawned and, after saying Mass and reciting the doctrine with my few Indians, we left the church. Even before I entered my room at about eight in the morning, the hostile Piatos Cimarrones [wild, rough, or runaway Pimas Altos] with the Seris and some Apaches (about twenty or thirty at most) fell on that unfortunate pueblo of Santa Magdalena. It seemed to me there were only about twenty whom I saw personally. Some were mounted and others on foot. They bore arrows, lances, and small oval shields. Some wore tanned hides like the soldiers'. All howled in unison and they caused such destruction that they destroyed the pueblo. The Indian women, with their small children, came running to my house for refuge. My Indians, who were only four or six, began to defend the pueblo. They could do little, however, against the infernal fury of such ferocious enemies and barely succeeded in saving their own lives.

The battle lasted about two hours. In three assaults they caused the following damage: in the first assault they seized the few horses I had for my needs and for traveling. (There were none at all in the pueblo.) They left me completely stripped and on foot. Then they took the few cattle and oxen belonging to the pueblo from the corral beside the house while we looked on, unable to prevent it. Then they began to sack the houses of the Indians and to set fire to them. After this, they retired to the brush for awhile in order to secure the cattle and other animals they had stolen. They came back the second time in a confused mob and continued the sack of the houses and the burning. One bold captain, an apostate named Juan Cozinero [John Cook], entered my house. It consisted of seven rooms in a row, one after the other. There was a kitchen, then a storeroom followed by two other rooms, and then another larger one which was a parlour. Finally, there were two medium-sized rooms. The whole was of adobe with a roof of grass and earth. He took fire from the kitchen and going up a ladder to the roof of the kitchen, he set fire to it. The house began to burn—the house which was my refuge and that of my few people. From there they went on to the church and, opening the door by force, they broke open the chest of vestments. They carried them all off without leaving a thread. They also took the holy chalice and the holy oil containers, spilling the holy oils. Besides this they ripped the linen from the statues and took a lovely image of San Francisco Xavier from its case. They threw it on the floor, breaking an arm. After having defiled and ruined the candlesticks, the baptismal font, and everything holy in the church, they retired a second time to the brush to secure the sacred things they had stolen. On the way they tore up the missal and threw away whatever they found cumbersome or which did not suit them.

Let us pause a moment at this second retreat; or rather, let us catch our breath to mourn over such a great misfortune. We watched the houses burn. The fire spread from the kitchen to the storeroom and to the two adjoining rooms. There remained only the large room and the two adjoining rooms where we were able to take refuge under cover of the smoke which was already bothering us. Finally, the hostiles returned for the third time. Their intent was to take our lives, for nothing else remained in the pueblo. My Indians were now only three archers with very few arrows, as they had used up all the rest. The enemy attacked the house. We shut ourselves up in the large room.

Here we were, with the fire near, without arms, and with the enemy at the door. This they struck three times with a great rock, making a fairly large hole in the middle. Through this opening my Indians shot their few arrows. At this the enemy withdrew a little, although remaining within sight. Now came the greatest agony, for either we would have to die indoors by fire, which was already beginning to spread to the parlour where I was with my Indians, or else, going outside we would have to give ourselves up to the enemy who would kill us with lances. If they should set fire to the heaps of grain in the last two rooms, even though the door was open, not one of us would escape alive. If they should attack the door again, which was already split, we would be unable to defend the entrance. I cried to God as best I could, and resigning myself to die, I waited for them to come in and deliver the final blow and end my life.

Suddenly, the enemy was in retreat! Just at that moment, Indians and others were arriving from San Ignacio [five miles away] to save us. An Indian who had fled from the skirmish had informed them of what was happening. Besides, the smoke of the con-flagration could be seen from San Ignacio. I came out of the parlour with my Indians, alive, thank God, or rather, revived. With the others I succeeded in extin-guishing the fire which was already in the parlour and kept the last two rooms from burning, thus saving a few books and some other things.

My agony was great at finding myself in the patio of the house and seeing the pueblo and houses burning, Indian women weeping, and at my feet a poor pregnant woman whom the enemy had caught and transfixed to the floor with their lances. Her little daughter's intestines were hanging out and she was dying. I confessed her and she died the following night. They took captive a married Indian woman with her two little sons and two infants. About noon, Father Zúñiga arrived. He had thought me dead. His coming was my greatest consolation. He brought me a horse and took me to San Ignacio where we arrived at three in the afternoon.

Episodes such as this described so vividly by Father Font occurred throughout the eighteenth century, although Piman participation in them dropped off sharply. Spaniards simply ignored the westernmost Papagos, and the mission at Sonoyta was never rebuilt after its destruction in 1751. Moreover, Papagos found themselves increasingly allied with Spaniards in a marriage of necessity forced by the increasing raiding and warfare by Apaches. Papagos, like Spanish settlers, were raising livestock by the last quarter of the 1700s. Their animals, not to mention their larders of agricultural products, presented tempting targets to the hunting-gathering and chiefly nonfarming Apaches. If Papagos were to protect themselves against these assaults, they could best do so with the support of Spanish firepower.

In 1782 Spaniards recruited and organized what turned out to be a highly successful company of Piman-speaking Indians for military service against Apaches and other enemies. Initially stationed at San Ignacio, this force and its successors worked throughout the Pimería Alta and its borders. In 1785 the company was transferred to the Sonoran *presidio* of Buenavista; in 1787 it was transferred to Tubac. Tubac, an O'odham settlement-turned-*presidio* in 1752, was no longer a fort when the Piman troops got there. The *presidio* had been moved to the O'odham village of Tucson in 1775–76, thus marking the beginnings of Tucson as a non-Indian metropolis.

The Piman Company at Tubac served long and well. In 1795 twenty-six of its members accompanied Captain José de Zuñiga on an expedition to New Mexico in an effort to open a direct Sonora-New Mexico route. The first quarter of the nineteenth century, through Mexican independence in 1821, saw these Piman soldiers involved chiefly in peaceful garrison duty.

It was at least ten years after Mexico had achieved her freedom from Spain before the Sonoran government got around to concerning itself officially with the Papagos. In 1831, decree number nineteen of the Sonoran constituent congress created two civil offices for each major Indian settlement in the Pimería Alta. The first was the *juez-económo*, a combination tribal judge and overseer of communal property. The second was that of *alguacil*, a constable to enforce law and order. Troubles between Papagos and Mexicans were springing up once more in the Altar Valley-Caborca area and farther west. Mexican prospectors and miners, drawn to the region by occasional strikes of gold and silver, arrived with little concern for Papagos' prior rights. And Mexican settlers, with their cattle and an appetite for irrigable farm lands, also shoved into this part of Papago country.

On April 1, 1832, the town council of Altar, the village founded as a *presidio* in 1754, petitioned the state government to create new native offices to centralize self-government in the Indian communities of Pimería Alta. They hoped this would stem increased Papago raiding. The council suggested the appointment of Enrique Tejada as "captain general of Pimería Alta," which included the lower Gila River. He was a Caborca Papago who for many years had been captain of the Sixth Infantry Company of Pimans. Because Tejada said he had no influence beyond the Caborca district, the council suggested Francisco Carro, a Papago from Saric, as his lieutenant with jurisdiction over the northern and eastern areas. These military leaders were to coordinate with local Papago judges and constables in punishing Papago raiders.

Tejada received the appointment, but his advanced age and poor health brought about his retirement in April 1835. Carro was made his successor.

To forestall a major uprising of Papagos, Mexicans created the office governor-general of all the Papagos and chose Antonio Salinas of Pirigua (Hickiwan) to fill the post. He was to work with Carro, then stationed in Caborca. Despite these appointments, matters continued to disintegrate with further gold discoveries and a further influx of Mexican rancher-farmers. An official of the town of Altar wrote to the governor of Sonora in April 1838:

> Apart from the numerous reports, I myself have been eyewitness to Papago discontent in such villages as Quitovac, Sonoyta, Carricito, Soñi, Arivaipa, and Cubó, because of insults and even extortions they have suffered at the hands of unscrupulous Mexican miners and because of the enormous amount of water taken from them to supply the mining camps and particularly in the lands acquired by Diego Celaya, which the Papagos consider as theirs by natural right of possession and residence there from time immemorial. There can be no doubt but what Papago discontent will increase as more and more water and land are taken from them.

The situation finally came to a head. In May 1840, more than a hundred Papagos fought a battle with Mexicans and their Papago allies at Cóbota, a village about midway between Poso Verde and Sonoyta just south of the present international boundary. Between then and June 1843, there were major military campaigns involving Papagos from the Cóbota area and other northwestern settlements versus Mexicans and Papago soldiers from Caborca and Pitiquito. Many Yaqui Indians who had been employed as laborers in the newly discovered mines defected and joined the Cóbota Papagos as allies.

Finally, in June 1843, weary of being pursued throughout most of the northern Sonoran Desert, the Papagos agreed to end hostilities. The third Piman Revolt came to a conclusion, with Gila River Pima chief Culo Azul acting as arbiter. The 1843 entry on a Papago calendar stick is succinct: "The peace was permanent." Almost, at least.

In June 1854, the United States and Mexico agreed to the Gadsden Purchase. Without consulting or informing the Indians of Pimería Alta, Washington and Mexico City cut their homelands in half. The northern portion became part of the territory of New Mexico (the territory of Arizona came into being in 1863), and the southern portion remained within the Estado de Sonora. Some Papagos, possibly as many as half of them, remained as Mexican citizens. The others fell into a kind of legal limbo that characterized the status of many American Indians in the United States at mid-nineteenth century. Papagos were neither regarded nor treated as citizens of the United States until all Indians in the country were given citizenship in 1924. This is in spite of the fact that "Mexicans" who chose to go on living in the Gadsden Purchase area for one year after treaty ratification on June 30, 1854, were "considered to have elected to become citizens of the United States." Whether Papagos qualified as "Mexicans" under terms of the treaty is an open question. Besides, Mexicans were to be admitted to citizenship "at the proper time (to be judged by the congress of the United States)." The proper time for Arizona's Papagos seems to have been 1924.

The effects of a new boundary between Sonora and Arizona were not immediate. The primary concern of Papagos and Mexicans alike who lived in the border area was the growing menace of raiding Apaches. In 1848 or very early in 1849 the Piman Indians still living at Tumacacori moved northward to the comparatve safety of San Xavier del Bac. The nearby *presidio* of Tucson still had a functioning military unit. Indeed, because it was the only such unit within more than a 150-mile radius, its enlisted men and officers remained in Tucson until 1856, more than a year and a half after it had become United States territory, to protect the local citizens agains Apaches as best it could. It was 1856 before the United States was able to send its own troops into the region.

How serious matters had become is indicated by the fact that by mid-nineteenth century, Tucson was the only Mexican settlement remaining in the northernmost reaches of the Sonoran Desert. San Xavier del Bac was the only Piman settlement left in the Santa Cruz Valley, discounting the Papagos living adjacent to Tucson. In the riverless desert to the west there were only Papago villages. Despite their seeming isolation, they, too, were fair game in Apache eyes. A calendar stick entry for 1852 provides a grim example:

Near the old abandoned mine called the Quijotoa was once a Papago village [called Nuestra Señora de la Merced del Batki by Father Kino, who visited the village in 1698]. It had been there for an unknown length of time. Situated in the beautiful foothills and hidden from invaders, it had nestled in prosperity throughout the centuries.

Near sundown one day in this year a member of the village reported to the chief that he had seen someone skulking nearby and examining the village from different places. The chief was not impressed and replied indifferently. Next morning the chief was informed that some people could be seen to the eastward. He was again unimpressed and said that it was probably other Papagos coming to visit the people of the village.

In a very few moments all could plainly see that it was a war party of the Apaches and their allies who had camped the night before nearby, and had sent a scout around the village to find out its strength and exact location.

Although surprised and heavily outnumbered, the Papagos prepared to give battle. They placed the old men, women, and children in a house and instructed them not to come out for any reason until the battle was finished. Then hastily arming themselves, they stoutly advanced to meet the enemy and attacked them with such fury that they drove them back a long distance to a deep wash where they entrenched themselves. The Papagos could not drive them out by storm, so they retreated in order to draw them out. The ruse was successful and the Papagos again drove them back. Again and again this was repeated until the Papagos lost so many men that they were content to stand and fight it out, which they did, to the last man.

The Apaches then proceeded to mop up. They killed the old men and burned the houses and all the property except such as they wished to take for spoil. They took the women and children and hurried homeward.

It is said that a few of the women escaped with their children to the mountains when it became evident that their men were fighting a losing battle.

The Apaches treated their captive women and children kindly, for, when peace was made with the Apaches years later, several of them were found alive and well. Asked if they wished to return to the Papagos, they replied in the negative.

Some of the Apaches and their allies had guns, and the neighboring villagers heard the noise of the battle. They hurried to the scene but arrived too late. They found all the warriors dead. However, they had the satisfaction to find many more of the enemy warriors dead.

Evidence was found to prove that four different tribes [bands?] of Indians composed the opposing force.

The pattern of Papago-Mexican military alliance against Apaches that had begun in the eighteenth century continued between Papagos and Americans in the United States in the nineteenth century. Papagos fought with

Americans as short-term enlistees in the army. They also fought against Apaches on their own or with American civilians. One such occasion was the "Camp Grant Massacre" of 1871, in which ninety-eight Papagos and fifty-four non-Indians from Tucson descended on presumably peaceful Apaches living on the San Pedro River. The raiders killed two men, about a hundred Apache women and children, and took twenty-seven Apache children captive.

Papago and Apache fighting, which seems to have begun only after Father Kino bestowed the attractive gift of horses and cattle on Pimans in the late seventeenth century, did not come to a halt until the final surrender of Geronimo in 1886. In two hundred years there grew such an enmity between these groups that it has taken nearly until the present before young Papagos have been willing to let bygones be bygones. Old people, who heard vivid tales of Apache woes from their parents and grandparents, still have not forgotten.

It was partly against the background of Apache warfare in southern Arizona that the United States developed its policy toward Papagos. They were perceived almost immediately as "allies" or "friendly" Indians by incoming Anglo-Americans. The entire history of three major Papago "rebellions," not to mention nearly constant skirmishing on the part of some Papagos, vis-à-vis Spaniards and Mexicans, was never considered by Anglo newcomers. Papagos were praised as never having fought against "whites," and they were characterized as a peaceful people, however bloodthirsty and personal their defensive and vengeful warfare against Apaches might be.

John Walker, who was appointed the first United States Indian agent to Indians of the Gadsden Purchase area in June of 1857, began almost at once bestowing federal largesse on Papagos. He supplied them with free shovels, hoes, brass kettles, butcher knives, scissors, saddlers' awls, needles, square axes, helves axes, steel shovel-plough points, tin cups, and spools of cotton. He hired a Vermont blacksmith to teach Papagos blacksmithing. And he defied instructions from the Superintendent of Indian Affairs in giving free flour to Papagos, nearly exhausting the entire supply for the whole New Mexico Superintendency in the process. It seemed impossible to Walker, who was from Tennessee, that Papagos could survive on "mescal [agave], tunies [prickly pear cactus fruit], and acorns."

New mines that were developed in the mountains next to the Santa Cruz Valley proved to be an attraction to Papagos. Many of them worked part time as laborers, and some sold agricultural and other products both to mines and to citizens in places such as a slowly growing Tucson. One important commodity was the salt Papagos collected at the head of the Gulf of California. In the late 1850s until the Civil War came to Arizona in the early 1860s, the mines at Tubac alone bought 20,000 pounds of Papago-collected salt each year.

There is little question that Papagos generally welcomed the coming of Anglo-Americans and the new regime of the United States to southern Arizona. Foremost among the reasons for such a welcome was the military potential of American troops and their ability to put a check on further Apache encroachments. Papagos also welcomed the development of mines and ranches, especially along the Santa Cruz Valley, where they could sell both goods and labor. Even to the west, closer to the heart of Papago country, mines such as those at Picacho, Fresnal, and Quijotoa, developed in the 1860s, '70s, and '80s, were viewed in a positive way. "Many Indians secured employment," was the 1867 calendar-stick entry concerning the Picacho mine, "obtaining money for their labor." Only in the far west, such as at Gu Wo (Kerwo) and Hickiwan, did Papagos actively resist white intrusion. In 1857 two American citizens lost their lives there, presumably at the hands of two Hickiwan Papagos who stole their five horses and some other goods.

In 1863, Arizona Territory's first Superintendent of Indian Affairs, Charles D. Poston, counted eighteen major Papago settlements and estimated the Papago population in the United States at 6,800. He warned that if the non-Indian population in the area should increase without a corresponding increase in the water supply, Indians would die.

Papagos repeatedly appealed to various Indian agents who were employed by the Department of the Interior to work among them to secure their land and water rights. Finally, in 1874 President U. S. Grant signed an Executive Order that withdrew about 71,000 acres of land around Mission San Xavier del Bac from the public domain, reserving it for the use and benefit of Papago Indians. In 1882, a second reservation was established for Papagos living on the Gila River at Gila Bend, Arizona. It was even smaller than the San Xavier Reservation: 22,400 acres.

If Papagos went to work in mines opening in their country, they also went to work on cattle belonging to whites invading their lands. Complaints lodged against Papagos for stealing cattle increased starting in the late 1870s. "The country between Tucson and the belt of country in which these mines are located—Papago Mining District—" noted a Tucson newspaper, "is fast filling up with herds of stock and ranchmen."

The government agent for the Pimas and Papagos, stationed at Sacaton on the Gila River (Pima) Indian Reservation, summarized the situation in 1887:

> [Papagos] have been able heretofore to prosecute and carry on this industry by reason of springs of water and wells at the foot of mountains, where there is fair grazing land. When the spring or well at one point becomes dry, or the grass exhausted, they drive their stock to another point, and only use their homes in villages a small portion of the year.
>
> This small privilege is fast being wrested from them, for the country is fast filling up with cattlemen (whites), and now at almost every spring or well some white man has a herd of cattle, and the inevitable result follows, the Indian is ordered to leave, and the "superior race" usually enforces such an order. The large scope of the country over which they are scattered, and the distance from this agency, ren-

ders it practically impossible for the agent to protect them against these wrongs, though I have traveled one hundred miles over a desert to secure an Indian the privilege of taking water from a well he had dug himself.

At long last, an Executive Order was issued by the president of the United States in January 1916 that created the Papago Indian Reservation generally in the form in which it exists today. Subsequent subtractions and additions, when combined with the already existing San Xavier and Gila Bend reservations, have made the Papago Reservation the second largest Indian reservation in the United States. Its approximately 2,800,000 acres make it second only to the Navajo Reservation in terms of land area.

By the time a large portion of their lands had been secured to them, Papagos had firmly adopted cattle raising as an important part of their economy. They had also seen the first deep water wells drilled in their country, with at least one Papago cattleman drilling his own wells. These marvels of industrial technology meant that it was no longer necessary to migrate seasonally from summer fields to winter wells. An underground source of water in the valley field settlements meant people could live in them year-round, and that is precisely what happened in many instances.

Papago horizons were expanded, and the people were drawn ever more away from the subsistence economy that had sustained them in the Sonoran Desert for generations. They were attracted by expanding markets for labor and goods in non-Indian communities surrounding Papago homelands; mining; the improvement in transportation to the outside world made possible by the arrival of the Southern Pacific railroad in Tucson in 1880; and the recruitment of Papago labor to harvest beets in Colorado and repair levees in Southern California.

Until the main Papago Reservation was established in 1916, most change brought about in the lives of Papagos by non-Indians was the result of the carrot rather than the stick. Deep wells, irrigation systems (at San Xavier), adobe houses, horses, cattle, wagons, markets for labor and produce, and desirable things that could be bought for cash—these were powerful inducements to change.

More direct efforts to bring about the assimilation of Papagos into the "mainstream" of American life—whatever that was—were carried out by Catholic nuns who opened a school at San Xavier in the 1870s, by Presbyterian missionaries who went to work in Papago country in the 1890s, and by Franciscan priests who again took up their cause among Papagos in the late nineteenth and early twentieth centuries. Presbyterians, Catholics, and the federal government—usually in competition with one another—labored to open boarding schools and day schools and to get Papago pupils into them. The government's Phoenix Indian School opened in 1891, and from then until now it has counted Papagos among its boarding students. In 1900 fifty-four Papagos were sent to an industrial training school in Grand Junction, Colorado, and the next year twenty-one Papagos went to school at Chilocco, Oklahoma.

Father Bonaventure Oblasser, a Franciscan who began to work regularly among Papagos in 1912, laid the foundations of a Papago day-school system when he began parochial elementary schools at the villages of Little Tucson (1912) and San Miguel (1914). Other priests started two other day schools in Papago country in 1914, one at Chuichu and another at Gila Bend. These were followed by similar schools at Cowlic (1915), Cababi (1915), and Anegam (1916). By 1916 the federal government had either completed or begun construction of day schools at Indian Oasis (Sells), San Miguel, Vaiva Vo (Cocklebur), Santa Rosa, Kohatk, Vamori, Chuichu, and Gila Bend.

A few Papago youngsters were also directly affected by the 1891 inauguration of the government's "outing system." This was a program in which female Indian pupils were given employment in non-Indian homes—chiefly as servants or domestics—as a means of bringing them into close and prolonged contact with the "civilizing" influence of non-Indians. Among other things, such contact was intended to help these girls learn English.

The remaining "stick" used in an effort to beat the Indianness out of Papagos in the pre-1917 era took the form of land allotment. In 1887, Congress passed a bill providing for individual, as opposed to community or tribal, ownership of land. This law, known as the Dawes Act, was passed in the belief that ". . . the enjoyment and pride of individual ownership of property is one of the most civilizing agencies." Until the passage of this bill, Papagos, like many American Indians, recognized that particular groups of people—whether dialect groups, villages, tribes, subtribes, et cetera—had rights to specific areas of land. Such rights, however, were not those of an individual. At the very least, they were rights of a family.

The General Allotment Act (Dawes Act) provided for the parcelling out of tribal lands on the basis of 160 acres to each head of household, 80 acres to single persons over eighteen and orphans under eighteen, and 40 acres to other single persons under eighteen. Married women, not being the "head of household," got nothing. If Indians failed to agree on the selection of lands among themselves, a special government allotting agent would be sent to make the division for them. Title to the allotments was placed in trust for a twenty-five-year period or longer, at the end of which time the allottee was to be given title in fee simple. With fee simple title he earned his United States citizenship and owned the real estate under precisely the same terms as any other citizen. It also meant he was then required to pay taxes on lands that formerly had been exempt from taxation because of their status in federal trust. "Surplus" lands on reservations remaining after all eligible Indians received allotments could be bought by the United States and disposed of as the government saw fit.

When the allotting agent arrived at the San Xavier Reservation in 1890, he counted 363 Papagos who were there at the moment. That some of them were possibly visiting there temporarily from villages to the west, or that other permanent residents were away at the moment, were practical matters that failed to concern him. Before he left he had drawn lines on a map of the reservation and put the names of individual Papagos on various squares. Ninety-four family heads got one hundred sixty acres each: twenty acres of farm land, from fifty to eighty acres of "timber" (mesquite) land, and the balance in so-called "mesa" land, good for nothing at the time except grazing cattle. He could not know that years later—starting in the 1950s—some of those "worthless" lands would prove to have large quantities of copper under them.

Each single person, depending on his or her age, got either forty or eighty acres of mesa land (no farm land or mesquite), and seventy-one wives of heads of household received no assignments. Some of the mesa land was deemed to be so poor that two acres were given for one. When the agent finished, there were about 41,600 acres of allotted land on the 71,090-acre reservation.

Papagos, who had virtually no understanding of what was being done in their behalf, merely continued to farm, graze cattle, cut mesquite for fuel, and to build their houses where they always had. The trust period was extended at the end of twenty-five years and extended again so that all the allotted lands at San Xavier continue in federal trust (and therefore remain tax exempt). None of the "surplus" lands at San Xavier were sold; these remain as Papago tribal lands.

Because the vast majority of Papagos have never written wills, each time a person with an interest in an allotment has died that person's heirs have been determined in accordance with Arizona succession laws. The acreage within the allotments has not been further subdivided, but the individuals' interests in those acres have been. The modern result is such unbelieveable fractionization that only the invention of electronic computers has made it possible to keep records of what Papagos have what percentage of interest in a particular allotment. One wag has commented that if the lands themselves were divided, and if one were to be buried on one's allotment, that person would have to be buried standing up. And at that, it would be a tight fit.

Papagos at Gila Bend were ignored in the allotting process. By the time the main reservation was created in 1916, flaws in the Dawes Act had become so apparent that the implementation of allotments was forestalled until it was finally dropped altogether. This means that most Papago lands are tribally, rather than individually, owned; all are held in trust by the federal government. Only at San Xavier are there allotments to complicate further the relationship between these original inhabitants of the Sonoran Desert and the rest of the world.

Missions, schools, outing programs, and paper land reform certainly did their share to assault Papago traditions and their conceptions of themselves before 1916. There is little doubt, however, that the deepest changes were those made willingly, if unwittingly, by Papagos who traded short-term gains for long-range consequences. The old man eating the white man's canned peaches in the trading post at Covered Wells was not aware of the hidden costs.

Blackwater

When shown on a map, which is not very often, the place is called Pozo Prieto, which means "Black Well" or "Blackwater" in English. Had there been a Papago there when we arrived in January 1980, he might have called it s-Cuk Ṣu:dagĭ. But there was nobody. There were just a few rangy cattle, one of them, a skinny Hereford, with a generous barbed stem of cholla cactus sticking to his nose.

The man who had directed us to the place, a veterinarian employed by Mexico's Instituto Nacional Indigenista (National Indian Institute), intimated that this was the southernmost Papago "settlement" in Sonora. A report published in 1965 shows another Papago locale, Pozo Grande (Big Well or Ge Wahia), still a little farther south. It apparently no longer qualifies as "Papago," however. Even as it was, the entire Papago population of Blackwater had gone to Caborca for the day, about thirty-five miles distant, and opinion had it he wouldn't be back until evening. His name was Felizardo Miranda Urbina, and he had been seen in Caborca earlier that same morning by one of the six of us paying a visit to his ranch.

We strolled around the ruins of Blackwater, taking pictures of desert scenery and of adobe structures in various stages of decay. Only one house, that belonging to Miranda, remained in good repair. The rest brought to mind images of a Papago ghost town, an historical village that was an archaeological ruin in the making.

While we walked around, the veterinarian was pleased to see a cow and her newborn calf who had been thought missing. Two other calves born a month or two earlier had swollen the size of Miranda's herd from thirty-seven to forty head. He was doing all right. And while his cattle may not have been very fat, the presence of the well from which Blackwater takes its name assured them of plenty to drink. It was enclosed by a large and handsome mesquite corral, one with at least ten to fifteen cords of wood in it.

In spite of Miranda's absence, it would have been premature to label Blackwater as an abandoned village. His house, cattle, well, and neatly maintained corral made it clear that "abandoned" is a relative concept in the world of Papago culture. "Temporarily not at home" is a closer description, especially if one understands that "temporarily" might mean anything from a day to two or three years. Carl Lumholtz, the great Norwegian naturalist who toured this part of the country in 1909–10, said Blackwater was visited seasonally by Papagos but that it was "more or less abandoned." So it was seventy years later.

To understand the contemporary situation among Mexican Papagos is not very difficult. This is partly because

María Valencia de García, Caborca, Sonora

there are fewer than 200 of them still living in Sonora. But it helps to know something about their history.

Danny Lopez, a Papago who makes it his business to learn about the history and traditional culture of his people, and I found ourselves standing on the brick roof above the portal of Mission San Ignacio one day. We had a splendid view of this veritable desert oasis from the top of the church. Father Kino himself had selected this site for a mission in 1687. It was a large O'odham settlement. The village plaza, the carefully aligned quiet dirt streets bordered by rows of adobe houses, and orchards of pomegranates, quinces, and citrus between the town and the river made an idyllic scene as Danny and I contemplated the view.

"How many Papagos live here now?" he wanted to know.

"Danny," I laughed, "this is a one-hundred-percent Mexican community. There haven't been any Papagos living here for at least a hundred years."

He was shocked. "None?"

"None."

"When I get back to Tucson and the reservation, I'm going to get a bunch of our kids and bring them down here and show them what can happen if they don't shape up."

In Father Kino's day, of course, Pimans, missionaries, and a few soldiers were the only human inhabitants of virtually all of what is now northwestern Sonora. Every settlement north and west of Kino's rim of Christendom all the way to the Río Gila belonged solely to Indians. But now? Now the Instituto Nacional Indigenista tallies six major Papago communities and nine smaller ones, or "annexes," still in Sonora. There is, moreover, irony in the tally inasmuch as it does not include Caborca, a growing Mexican metropolitan center lying in the heart of a booming industrial farming area (thanks to the pumping of underground water supplies). And it is in Caborca, not to mention the non-Indian towns of Sonoyta and Rocky Point, that as many as 150 of Sonora's approximately 200 Papagos live most of the time. Although scattered through-

Amelia Chihiva, Caborca, Sonora

out the city, most of their homes are on "K" Street between First and Second Avenues.

The preemption of Papagos' waterholes and lands began long before the international boundary halved traditional territory in 1854. The collapse of the mission system in the 1830s, gold and silver discoveries, and an influx of Mexican settlers from the south combined to bring pressures on Papagos they were unable militarily to withstand. Warfare of the early 1840s ended essentially in the Papagos' defeat. Their choice was either to find some accommodation with Mexicans via assimilation or by laboring for Mexicans on the latters' terms or to withdraw more deeply into the riverless desert to the north. Many O'odham, no doubt, chose withdrawal.

No one has yet done a careful historical study of the fate of Sonoran Papagos during the last half of the nineteenth century. It is clear from many travelers' accounts, however, that after the 1850s such former Papago settlements as Cocospera, Imuris, San Ignacio, and Magdalena were basically non-Indian in their makeup. Farther to the west along the Río Altar and at Pitiquito and Caborca, Papagos continued to live. But as the nineteenth century wore on, they found themselves living as members of a minority population surrounded by more powerful and affluent Mexicans. Mexican law, moreover, did not recognize any special "Indian" status. Indians were, and are, regarded as Mexican citizens on a par with everyone else. Papagos received no reservations or land titles by virtue of their "Indianness."

Saric, a Sonoran trouble spot for non-Papagos since the late seventeenth century, persisted in this role for more than 150 years. A Tucson, Arizona, newspaper, basing its report on admittedly hearsay evidence, printed an account in May 1878, saying that Felix Bustamente of Saric had caught two Papagos stealing his cattle. He shot one of them; the other got away. A large party of Papagos subsequently attacked Bustamente's ranch and killed him in revenge. The report continued that Mexican troops had been summoned and that some 2,000 Papagos were camped nearby waiting to attack. The figure, if true at all, was surely highly inflated. Nor is there further word in later editions of the newspaper that anything more happened.

At the time of Father Kino's death in 1711, the southern boundary of Papago territory seems roughly to have been marked by the Concepción and Magdalena rivers. There may have been a few settlements within an area as much as twenty-five miles south of these rivers, but here one encountered the northern limits of Seri Indian country.

In the late 1870s and early 1880s, the Sonora Limited railroad was constructed along the 260-mile distance between the seaport of Guaymas, Sonora, and Nogales, Arizona, tying these neighboring states together with iron bands. Although the route followed by the tracks was an ancient one, the railroad spawned new settlements and new commerce along its right-of-way. In all probability, Papagos worked as laborers in the construction of the road that was joined to the tracks of the Santa Fe Company's line in Nogales in October 1882. A dozen years later, when W. J. McGee, a Smithsonian Institution ethnologist, traveled south by wagon paralleling the railway, he found two families of Papagos living permanently at a place south of Llano and "four or five families" living at Querobabi with "a headman or chief, who inherited his office; he is now an old man. There is no 'doctor,' and in case of illness a shaman is called from one of the settlements in the next valley westward."

On October 25, 1894, McGee noted in his field diary:

> No Papago at Santa Ana. . . . At Santa Marta, a league below San Lorenzo, there formerly dwelt continuously a family of Papago, which was a nucleus for a nomadic group; but the son shot the father in a domestic difficulty some years ago, and the family were scattered, a part going to Caborca. A group of Yaki [Indians] were at Santa Ana loafing around the [railroad] station.

Between Querobabi and Hermosillo, the capital of Sonora, McGee found no more Papago settlements. But in Hermosillo he learned of a ranch called Chanati, about six miles below the city, where some fifteen Papagos in three families lived in two houses. He also heard about El Pozito, a ranch four or five miles to the south comprised of eight families. He said the people at Chanati "do not farm. The men work occasionally for 'the Governor,' chiefly as *vaqueros* [cowboys], but subsist principally by hunting. The women make ollas for sale in addition to domestic duties."

The people at El Pozito, on the other hand, "plant corn, melons, squashes, etc., on which, with mesquite beans and the like they commonly subsist; but in case of drought they work for or beg from the neighboring ranches, moving their habitation temporarily in order to do so more efficiently."

On his return trip, which took him more directly across the desert from Hermosillo to Altar, McGee found Papago families living at mining camps at places called Poso Nuevo and Ciénega, both still on maps of modern Sonora. His field diary gives us a good description of what were probably fairly typical late nineteenth-century Sonoran Papago households:

At Ciénega proper there are two groups of Papago Indians with another at "the other town." The first group occupy three houses N.W. of town; they are peons, at work in placers, the women making pottery: six in all, a father & mother, two grown sons, a nearly grown girl and a little girl. Two of the houses are of wigwam pattern made of sagebrush [i.e., *Larrea divaricata*] on poles, one with earthen covering, the other with debris on top—chaff of some sort, with corn husks, etc., evidently designed as a sort of substructure for an earthen covering when it became convenient to put it on. The third house is large, evenly circular, of sage-brush, with no roof. One of the women had been making pottery, and the tools of her trade were lying about. The other was making squash ready for cooking (in the rinds) and the seeds were ready for grinding. The elder woman was combing the hair of the sleeping little one, using a yucca brush. The other group, in S. pt. of town, is larger though living in a half-subterranean house inherited from some unknown builder probably Yaki. There are two middle aged women, with a half-grown girl and 4 or 5 smaller children. They were making pottery, being engaged in burning a kiln; the girl was washing a mantilla. One of these women wore sandals; all others seen were barefoot. Here, too, the men are placer peons. The father in the other group owes $60, one of the sons (who dined with us) $50, the debt being incurred in outfitting for work, and the more they work the deeper the debt becomes.

[José] Lewis visited the other settlement of Ciénega 2 mi. S. of the main town, finding there 6 families of Papago, all working in mines under peonage; and learning of still another group of two families, 2 mi. farther away, similarly under bondage. All of these Ciénega families, except perhaps the newest comers, are of doubtful purity of blood; most speak Yaki, and intermarry freely with the Yaki. . . .

Moving northward toward the international boundary, McGee found a Papago family "living Mexican" and "working sporadically on a ranch" at La Berruga, south of Caborca. As for Caborca, which he reached on November 12, 1894, McGee wrote:

How the mighty are fallen! Caborca has been for weeks [of the McGee expedition] a Mecca as a great Papago town, the Papago metropolis of Mexico! And there are two rancherias, one of five families at present, the other none! It is true that there is also a "temporal" [farming area] a dozen miles downriver [probably Las Calenturas], where there are half a dozen families, chiefly from Caborca. In winter there may be so many as a score of families here, though commonly some of the people are absent hunting.

Considering that the purpose of McGee's 1894–95 trip was to visit Papagos and to write a description of their culture, it is not hard to imagine his disappointment when he discovered that Caborca, reputedly the Papago capital of Sonora, was nearly devoid of Papagos. And remembering, too, that he was hoping to find Papagos who were the least acculturated, it is easy to sympathize with his further disappointment when he learned that one of the Caborca Papagos, a ten-year-old girl, had spent a year in the Phoenix Indian School, a federally operated boarding school in Arizona.

During the rest of his trip in Sonora, McGee found two households of Papagos at Pitiquito, both of whose "customs are essentially Mexican," and one Papago family living permanently at Altar. He also heard about Papagos living at Oquitoa, Quitovac, and Sonoyta, "a good many at either place."

The ethnologist's hopes of finding "aboriginal" Papagos in Mexico in 1894 were severely dashed. What he found instead were scattered groups of families, many of whom were already fully dependent on the Mexican economy for their subsistence. The people wore Mexican clothes; there was intermarriage, especially, it seems, with Yaqui Indians; there were no signs of social or political cohesiveness among these scattered segments of the Papago population. It appears that by 1894 the vast majority of Sonoran Papagos had either become thoroughly Mexicanized or had moved northward across the international boundary into the United States.

In April 1898, an incident occurred at the little mining town of El Plomo, about thirty-five miles south of Arizona, reminiscent of the 1878 affair at Felix Bustamente's ranch north of Saric. A Papago headman from the village of Cababi (Ge Wahia), Sonora, was jailed in El Plomo for having shot a Mexican's horse and for nonpayment of money owed for a cow. A rescue party of as many as forty Papagos, most of them from settlements in southern Arizona, attacked El Plomo in a vain attempt to rescue their jailed friend and relative. He and a few of the attackers were killed during the raid; the others fled north of the border, subsequently to be arrested, tried, and acquitted in United States federal court. At the time of the attack there were Papagos living at El Plomo, the men working as woodcutters. They chopped mesquite used to stoke a furnace that heated steam boilers for powering the ore crusher in the mill. After April 1898, they moved away. So, apparently, did a great many other Papagos still living in northernmost Sonora. There was no fence to hinder travel over the Sonora-Arizona line. By foot, horseback, and in wagon, growing numbers of O'odham spread into the southern portions of what years later was to become the Chukut Kuk (Owl Hoot) District of the Papago Indian Reservation.

In 1909–10, Carl Lumholtz was commissioned by "some influential friends" to make a study of the Papaguería, so he took up where McGee had left off. And unlike McGee, who never wrote a book about Papagos, Lumholtz put his notes into a volume first published in 1912, New Trails in Mexico.

During his wanderings among Papago settlements on both sides of the border, Lumholtz located an old man who kept a calendar stick. The annual events noted on the stick were narrated, and Lumholtz wrote them down. The stick gives an additional reason Papagos abandoned such settlements as Magdalena, San Ignacio, and Imuris: attacks by Apache Indians. In 1850, 1854, 1861, and 1862 there were fights between Papagos and Apaches at Magdalena, Santa Ana, and elsewhere in Mexico.

Lumholtz found eight Papago families living at Caborca, "most of them making their living by working for the Mexicans. . . . Few of the Indians here, however, can be depended upon for work, as they are demoralized by mescal brandy. They seem to employ their time between earning money and getting drunk therewith. They are no longer able to keep up their native feasts and are rapidly disappearing into the body of Mexican laborers. The same is the case with the remnants of Papagoes [sic] who live in the rest of the towns or settlements along the Altar River."

Before the end of his journey in Papago country, Lumholtz enumerated seventy-two Papago settlements, including winter and summer villages and "camps" of the Sand Papago (Soba) Indians. Of these, only twenty-three were any longer inhabited by Papagos, allowing for errors occasioned by seasonal movements. The majority of the seventy-two places he lists are annotated by such comments as, "Papago camp, abandoned; formerly of importance"; "The Papagoes used to have fields here. The old men died and the young men went to Arizona"; and "Mexican Pueblo, formerly rancheria." He estimated about 180 "families" still spending at least part of the year in Sonora. Figuring five persons to the family, this would make a 1909–10 Sonoran Papago population of 900—probably not too far from the truth. It would also suggest that from 3,000 to 4,000 Papagos had disappeared from Sonora throughout the nineteenth century.

Lumholtz made it clear there was continuing enmity between Mexicans and Papagos. He said of La Nariz, a Papago village just south of the Arizona line, that "in the winter usually fifteen families live here. At the time of my visit in November there were five families; some were absent in Represa de Enrique, others were working for the Americans (agriculture) in Arizona. There is a dam here made by Mexicans, American citizens, who are trying to drive the Indians away." And regarding Pozos de San Ignacio, about forty miles south of Caborca, "this rancheria was given up in 1907 after a brave fight with the *rurales* (Mexican police), of whom eighteen were killed, nearly all the Indians escaping with their belongings into Arizona. Many families were living here, sixteen persons being full-grown men."

Although Lumholtz did not visit Poso Verde, he described it as "the largest ranchería [of Papagos] in Sonora. Twenty-five to thirty families are said to live here." And he further noted, "There is a general here in charge of all the Papagoes in Sonora," doubtless the Papago governor general, the heir to the position that had been created by Mexicans in the 1830s.

Unlike McGee, Lumholtz spent a considerable amount of time exploring northwesternmost Sonora and the Pinacate Mountains. This area had been home for the so-called Sand Papagos, some of whom, at least, were included among the Soba of Father Kino's time. Although Lumholtz was able to identify by name some twenty Sand Papago camps, he could find only one Papago who continued to live in this nearly waterless region. This was Juan Carajavales, a Papago hermit who continued to live in a brush structure at Papago Tanks in the Pinacate mountains. Lumholtz referred to him as "the lonely Indian of the Pinacate. . . . Once a year he visits Sonoita to see relatives and to get drunk."

The Mexican Revolution of 1911 not only swept Porfirio Díaz, the dictatorial president, from power, but it led to a new constitution's being adopted in 1917. One of the major planks in the platform of social justice involved agrarian land reform, the protection of property rights for the "little people," i.e., small farmers and small ranchers as opposed to the big landowners. Exercising his authority under Article 27 of the 1917 Mexican constitution, President Elías Calles, by a proclamation signed April 12, 1928, created the *ejido* of the Congregación de Pozo Verde, giving the Papago Indians at Poso Verde community rights—in writing—to at least a portion of their aboriginal lands, some 2,832 hectares (ca. 7,675 acres). Other Sonoran Papagos seem not to have done so well; there is no record of any additional *ejidos* having been created.

In 1957 anthropologist Alfonso Fabila of Mexico made a report on Sonoran Papagos for the Instituto Nacional Indigenista. He counted eleven major Papago settlements and estimated a total Papago population of 745. He noted that Papagos in Sonora were living at subsistence level and that they raised few cash crops. He also noted that many Sonoran Papagos had relatives living and working in the United States.

Six years after Fabila's visit to the Papaguería, another anthropologist, Margarita Nolasco A., made a survey of Sonoran Papagos in behalf of Mexico's outstanding new Museo Nacional de Antropología in Mexico City. She and a photographer took pictures, compiled data, and collected a few artifacts for the museum. She counted 450 Papagos still living in Sonora, writing in her published report that Mexico's 1900 census had given a figure of 859; the 1930 census, 535; the 1940 census, 91 monolingual speakers of Papago; and a 1943 census, 505 Papagos, without saying how "Papago" was defined. The official 1950 and 1960 federal censuses included Papagos under the rubric of "others," making it impossible to say how many "others" were actually O'odham. Most Papagos in 1963 were bilingual in Papago and Spanish; a few could speak Papago, Spanish, and English.

Nolasco identified twenty Sonoran localities occupied, when at all, totally by Papagos. She distinguished nine additional places where Papagos either lived as a minority community (such as Caborca) or occupied the area only temporarily.

In 1975, the *Instituto Nacional Indigenista*, commonly known as INI, opened its *Residencia Papago*, an office for Sonoran Papago Indian affairs, in Caborca. Activity in this federal office grew, and in 1979 a new census was taken in an effort to delineate the office's clients and their principal problems. Investigations were carried out by a staff that included people with training in law, economics, social welfare, and anthropology. The census completed at the end of 1979 indicated a little fewer than 200 Papagos still living in Sonora. It was discovered, however, that a large number of Sonoran Papagos were living in Arizona, many of them having migrated there several years before.

Angelita García, San Pedro, Sonora

Alberto Celaya, San Pedro, Sonora

They were found living in farming communities on an arc surrounding—but not on—the Papago Indian Reservation. Many had married and raised families while living in the United States. Few of them expressed any immediate desire to return to Mexico in spite of promises that they would be made secure in their lands.

The six major Papago communities identified by the personnel of INI in 1979, and their annexes, were Las Norias (annexes: Santa Elena and El Carricito); El Bajio, also known as Carmelo or Many Dogs (annexes: El Cumarito, El Cubabi, and La Mochonera); San Francisquito (annex: El Carrizalito); Pozo Prieto or Blackwater (annex: Las Calenturas); Quitovac (annex: El Chujubabi); and the *ejido* of Poso Verde.

In 1980, INI opened a boarding school for Papagos at Quitovac, one which included a Papago teacher instructing Papago children, now monolingual in Spanish, in their native language. It is too early to say what the outcome of this experiment will be. It is similarly too early to predict how many Sonoran Papagos may return to Sonora with the promise of help from government programs and of inviolate land tenure.

The present governor general of the Papagos in Sonora, C. Rafael Alfonso García Valencia, lives in Caborca with other members of his family. As El Gobernador General de la Tribu Papago, this young man has taken his duties seriously. He has met with virtually all Papagos in Sonora, going to frequent meetings; he has traveled in Arizona, talking with Papagos in the United States; he has represented the Papagos at national meetings in Mexico City and elsewhere. Like the officials of INI with whom I spoke, he agrees that the biggest single problem facing Sonoran Papagos is that concerning their land, which continues to be encroached upon by more aggressive Mexican neighbors, both cattlemen and farmers. INI has given the Papago survivors new hope, but in the meantime the Papago response continues to be one more of resignation than otherwise. People work on their little farms or ranches for awhile; they sell their labor to Mexicans; they go to the

*Rafael García Valencia, El Gobernador General
de la Tribu Papago, Sonora*

bright lights of Caborca and stay for weeks or months until their money is spent or until they tire of it. Many Papagos are now married to Mexicans; their offspring speak only Spanish, and they learn next to nothing concerning traditional Papago cultural values or history. There are those, like Rafael García and many INI officials, who decry what has taken place and what continues to occur with respect to a "loss of Papago culture." But for Papagos who have chosen intermarriage and cultural assimilation, the process appears to have been relatively painless. And more importantly, it does appear to have been a choice on the part of individuals rather than the result of some plan to force cultural integration. That people would choose to leave small, isolated farms and ranches to lose themselves in cities is by no means unique among Papagos in Mexico. It is part of a worldwide trend. The countryside, now farmed by machinery rather than hands and driven by the desire for cash rather than the need for subsistence, is being forsaken for the presumed advantages of urban living. That there may be disastrous consequences of such a trend—recalling that industrial farming depends on fossil fuels for its perpetuation—is beside the point. It certainly is of no concern to a Papago now living in Caborca whose standard of living is on a par with that of most Mexicans in the city—which is the case with many Papagos.

While the threatened loss to Mexico of Papagos on their maps of indigenous peoples may constitute a prick in the Mexican national conscience, the Papagos involved view their disappearance—if they do, indeed, ultimately disappear—as natural and without trauma.

With land, however, it is another matter. Papagos deserve to be protected in their rights to land just as any other Mexican citizen, whether poor or rich. And INI's people are working hard to ensure those rights, often in the face of politically powerful opposition. With the installation of heavy-duty underground pumps in northwestern Sonora, the value of agricultural and grazing lands has soared in the past decade. Where there was once nothing but creosote bush, there are now thousands of acres of cotton, grains, and even vineyards, the grapes going into brandy production. Will Papagos be able to withstand the resultant pressures?

Parts of Sonora remain important to all Papagos for purely spiritual or religious reasons. Those parts are Magdalena and Quitovac. At one time salt deposits near the head of the Gulf of California had religious as well as economic significance for Papagos, with overland expeditions by foot to visit the ocean and to gather salt being one means by which young Papago males became grown men. Such expeditions, however, have not been held for at least forty years, and the ocean and salt on its shores are important as memories in cultural tradition and as identity symbols rather than as present realities.

Every year, either in late July or during August, Quitovac comes alive once more as a Papago settlement. O'odham from Sonora as well as a great many people from Ajo and the southwestern quarter of the Papago Reservation are drawn there to celebrate the Wi:gita ceremony.

One version has it that this particular ceremony started on instructions from Montezuma, the western Papagos' equivalent of the central and eastern Papagos' I'itoi. Montezuma killed a great water monster who had been devouring O'odham living in the region. He cut the monster's heart into two parts, carving one to represent a male and the other a female. Montezuma then held a great fiesta to celebrate the death of the monster, a grand celebration to which all the people were invited. He showed the O'odham how to care for the male and female objects and instructed them to hold a feast every year. Someone subsequently stole the male image, but as of 1920 when the ceremony was seen and described by Edward H. Davis, the female one was still being cared for.

In addition to commemorating the death of the creature who killed people, the ceremony, a religious dance drama, is a prayer for abundant rain, good crops, lush desert growth, health, and long life for the members of each family. Should the observance be neglected, the result might be floods, drought, sickness, or death.

When Davis witnessed the Wi:gita, ceremonial paraphernalia included deerskin masks worn as hoods and
from whose lower edges hung long fringes; sashes of bright-
colored fabric; necklaces of blue glass beads and shell
beads; bunches of eagle feathers; robes; anklets girdled
with cocoons filled with fine sand; and girdles of deerskin
from which were suspended several bells and seashells
strung on deerskin thongs. The event got under way with
the blessing of the house of Quitovac's headman, a bene-
diction that involved the sprinkling of sacred corn meal
on four little piles of sand that had been made in front of
the house.

The actual ceremony took place, as it does today, at a
ceremonial ground about a quarter of a mile away from
the spring-fed pond for which Quitovac is locally famous.
It started after sundown and lasted all night and all the
next day and involved singing, much of it to the accompaniment of men running sticks over notched rasps resting on inverted basket resonators. It also involved a ritual
speech about Montezuma and the origin and purpose of
the ceremony, as well as dancing by masked clowns and
men wearing eagle feather headdresses. Sacred corn meal
was sprinkled in holes made at the cardinal points; there
was a mock hunt for wild game and a mock roasting and
eating of caterpillars; and there was a parading of a white
cloth, symbolizing clouds, as a means of bringing rain.
The conclusion of the formal part of the ceremony was
followed by what Davis called "the grand debauch," the
all-night consumption of wine fermented from saguaro
cactus fruit. Every male was summoned to drink. Wrote
Davis:

> ... This could not be disregarded. The summons was
> always accompanied with the ceremonial phrase,
> "You are a good man when you are drunk." Any man
> so summoned rose immediately, found his way to
> the place of debauchery, and drank. Often the men
> would vomit, then proceed to drink again, and this

might happen several times during the night. All drank, both men and boys, until there was not a sober one in the village.

He estimated that 120 gallons of saguaro wine were consumed in one night. And unlike today, he said of the 1920 occasion, "During the drinking there was neither quarreling nor fighting."

The "debauch" observed by Davis had several functions. Botanist Frank Crosswhite, in describing the saguaro wine feast traditionally held by many Arizona Papagos, had this to say:

[Jack] Waddell (1973: 227) thought that the wine ritual "communicates the significance of egalitarianism, of sharing, of meeting reciprocal obligations, and of curbing aggressive behavior toward one's kinsmen that new forms of behavior evoke."

. . . Drinking the wine was a sacramental communion bringing good and purification to the communicant. It brought a supernatural presence and an ability for every Indian to call for rain. Singing brought power and was a supplication to the supernatural for rain.

. . . Papago wine-drinking filled the participants with liquid from the skyward reaches of the Saguaro which symbolically united with the earth when vomiting occurred.

Vomiting wine on the ground completed the cycle, returning moisture to the ground that had been taken up by the roots of the Saguaro, stored in its body during the time of drought, incorporated into the fruit, and made into the wine. Underhill (1946: 41) explained the ceremonial wine-drinking as symbolic, the Papago having had the idea "that the saturation of the body with liquor typifies and produces the saturation of the earth with rain." Further, the drunkenness and dizziness supposedly symbolized the pulse of a dizzy storm cloud with impending rain.

The first time John Schaefer and I visited Quitovac was early in August 1979. The spot, about two miles south of a paved highway, is surely one of the most idyllic in northwestern Sonora. A deep *charco*, or pond, has been excavated to trap the fresh water still pouring forth from a series of adjacent springs. Everything is perpetually green around the edges of the pond, a veritable desert oasis. Only one Papago household near the pond was still occupied, the home of Luciano Noriego and his family. Other houses were in ruins or abandoned.

We were two weeks late for that year's Wi:gita ceremony. Several days before our arrival, in late July, there had been a large crowd of Papago visitors from both sides of the border. It had rained since; the ceremony had been a success.

Señor Noriego kindly guided us to the ceremonial ground. Remnants of a ramada and other brush structures that had served their ceremonial purpose were still in evidence. So were dozens, perhaps hundreds of empty beer cans—largely Tecate brand. Something more than saguaro fruit wine had been drunk. Indeed, it is possible there had been no saguaro fruit wine at all, merely a "debauch," as Davis would have said. In recent years the Quitovac Wi:gita has earned the reputation—whether justified or not I cannot say—of being merely a pale reflection of its former self, a ceremony whose form has partially survived but whose content includes brawls as well as drunkenness that has little to do with bringing rain.

Luciano had spent virtually his whole life living near Quitovac. He had been born here. Many of his relatives, perhaps most of them, were living in Arizona. He told us that once he rode in a car for two and a half days to some large Mexican city to attend an Indian meeting. He didn't know the name of the city, but he had been impressed by its very, very tall buildings. "They sure must know how to make long sticks," he said, since all of Papago architecture is dependent on the length of sticks for its size.

Luciano shared with us some ripe fruit from his large fig tree. We ate them, with thanks, and drove off for

Tucson, another city whose buildings have long sticks.

The Sonoran Mecca for nearly all Papagos is the city which today is officially called Magdalena de Kino. Kino had called it Santa María Magdalena de Buquivaba; a mission visiting station was built possibly as early as 1690. In 1711, Kino died and was buried here, only to be uncovered by archaeologists in 1966. His skeletal remains, still *in situ*, are under glass and on public display surrounded by an entire tile-covered memorial plaza. The city that Kino named has added his name to its own.

Magdalena is one of two major pilgrimage centers in Sonora, the other being Aduana in the southern part of the state. The focal point for pilgrims visiting Magdalena is a life-size wooden gessoed and painted statue of St. Francis—a kind of generalized St. Francis, as it turns out. Although the reclining statue, kept in a chapel in the city's major church, is clearly intended to represent St. Francis Xavier, the great Jesuit saint, copies of this statue as well as depictions of it show it clothed in the brown habit worn by modern Franciscans. Moreover, the fiesta held annually in honor of St. Francis takes place on October 4 (and the two weeks preceding it), the feast day of St. Francis of Assisi, the founder of the Order of Friars Minor (Franciscans). San Francisco Xavier's feast day is December 3.

If this is confusing to an intellectual purist, it is of virtually no moment at all to the literally thousands of people who visit the statue of St. Francis in Magdalena each year, most of them in late September and early October. These thousands of people, firm in traditional aspects of their Catholic faith, include Yaqui Indians, Mayo Indians, Lower Pima Indians, Papago Indians, and Mexicans from both sides of the border. In fact, when it comes to the October 4 Feast of San Francisco de Asís, there might as well be no border.

To all these pilgrims, most of whom go to Magdalena in search of good health for themselves or their families, St. Francis is St. Francis. Whether Xavier or Assisi, Jesuit or Franciscan, is beside the point.

It is clear that Father Kino introduced the devotion of

San Francisco Xavier to Magdalena. When Kino died in 1711, he was there to dedicate a new chapel that had just been built to honor his favorite saint. It was inside this chapel, on the gospel side of the altar, that he was buried and where he was found by archaeologists 254 years later. San Francisco Xavier remained an important part of religious life in Magdalena after Kino's death. It will be recalled from Father Font's harrowing account of the attack made on Magdalena in 1776 that "a lovely image of San Francisco Xavier" was one of the items the attacking Indians desecrated, throwing it on the floor and breaking its arm.

It was probably sometime late in the eighteenth century, after Franciscans had replaced Jesuits in Pimería Alta, that a devotion to San Francisco Xavier came to be confused with a devotion to San Francisco de Asís. Documents indicate that the fiesta was still being properly observed in Magdalena on December 3, 1814, but by midcentury the date had switched to October 4. From an 1828 document we also learn that the Magdalena image of St. Francis, presumably a statue rather than a picture, had become the "object of devotion of all this upper part of the State of the West," that is, of modern Sonora.

One of the most vivid descriptions ever written concerning the Magdalena fiesta was penned by a French observer in the 1850s. Charles de Lambertie published it in 1855:

> A type of marketplace of palm fronds shelters the pyramids of various fruits of the tropics and the refreshing infusions of pineapples, lemon and citron. Around this rustic canopy rises a multitude of huts and branches, and between swirls the smoke first lit under the iron tripods which serve to prepare dishes in the open air, where, thanks to the influx attracted by the festival, one could starve while spending much money.
>
> The metallic tinkling of ounces and centavos reaches the curious who interrupt a moment their

promenade in order to be able to contemplate the piles of gold and silver which the audacious players hazard upon one card in *monte* [a card game].

But all that one had seen during the day was unable to give a pale idea of the magic spectacle which the pueblo afforded at nightfall. The candles, enclosed in paper lanterns of all colors, shone upon the·two rows of tables which lined the two sides of the principal streets. Upon these tables were found all that which the most refined Epicurean might desire in milk shops, pastry shops and candy shops. Over all these food dishes fluttered a multitude of little paper banners painted with all tints, which enhanced their air of display, and the pyramids of flowers cut with the vegetables, which would not have dishonored the Parisian taste, enhanced the symmetry of the women vendors.

With few changes, this description of the fiesta at Magdalena would serve nicely today. The town and its very modern statue of San Francisco Xavier continue to attract pilgrims and party goers each late September and early October. As the French author commented, "Piety was the pretext, but pleasure was the goal."

In reality, however, it is more than either piety or pleasure that brings the multitudes from afar on foot, by train, on horseback, and in cars, buses, and trucks. It is also hope, hope that a visit to the reclining statue of San Francisco will bring good health and recovery from illness or other afflictions. While merchants of all kinds abound, including salesmen of pots, pans, blankets, paintings, phonograph records, beer, soft drinks, and every imaginable kind of food, and while the atmosphere is one of a carnival, the real emphasis of the fiesta is on curing. Amid the fortune tellers and gambling games, merry-go-rounds and Ferris wheels, and booths with jewelry and plastic flowers, there are mountains of religious images: statues, holy pictures, scapulars, rosaries, printed tracts, crucifixes. So are there all kinds of healing herbs and dried animals, particularly invertebrate sea creatures. Vendors sell these herbal wares, displaying them with signs attached to explain the maladies for which each type is best. The list is an endless one.

Miraculous cures are said to have been brought about by the San Francisco statue. It is even possible to borrow some of the statue's power by holding one's own religious artifact—a statue, picture, rosary, or crucifix—against the reclining figure. As one Papago who took his small statue of St. Francis to Magdalena each year explained, "It's kind of like getting your battery recharged."

These holy images, most of which were purchased in Magdalena in the first place, make their way back to private shrines inside homes or to local churches and chapels. The Papago Reservation is dotted with such chapels whose altars and retables are covered with pictures and other objects that have the power of Magdalena's St. Francis in them. More than half the homes are similarly enriched.

In times gone by, Papagos who could not reach Magdalena by horse or wagon did so on foot. But today, all Papagos can either drive to Magdalena or get a ride with friends or relatives. Those people seen walking along the highway in September or October are almost exclusively Mexicans, rather than Papagos, who have made a vow or promise to walk the entire distance. This can mean as many as the sixty-five miles from Mexico's Nogales to Magdalena, or even farther. Such pilgrims are carrying out a penance in hopes of absolution or cure for themselves or a loved one. Or they are walking in thanks for a cure already effected.

The most important part of any trip to Magdalena, but not the most time-consuming, involves the visit to the statue. People touch it, kiss it, and even bite it. They also place a hand under his head and lift him slightly, something one can do only if one is in a state of grace.

The modern pilgimage to Magdalena continues to combine virtually all of the features of an eleventh-century pilgrimage to some European shrine. There are piety and pleasure, priests and panderers, hopes and hostilities,

*The Sacred Heart, a Papago shrine near
San Vicente Well in Arizona*

*Shrine of Our Lady of Guadalupe, near
White Horse Pass, Arizona*

miracles and maledictions. Geoffrey Chaucer's characters enroute to Canterbury would find themselves right at home among the Papagos and Mexicans.

Despite the glamor of Magdalena and its importance as a Papago shrine, and regardless of the romance of a native religious observance that manages to survive in Quitovac, the real story of Sonora's Papagos—in the final analysis—seems to be the story of Blackwater. It concerns Blackwater's tiny herd of cattle, its ruined buildings, and its gone-to-Caborca caretaker. It is the saga of "hanging on" culturally, physically, and economically in the face of history and against what appear to be overpowering odds.

Saltshaker

Papago Indian pottery comes close to being a relic of the past. When three fellow students and I did a survey and wrote a book on the subject in the late 1950s, we succeeded in identifying thirty-eight women who still made traditional earthenware bowls and jars. One potter, Laura Kermen of Topawa, also made figurines that she fired in an electric kiln.

Most Papago pots are made by molding a lump of wet clay over the base of another pot to form the lower half of the vessel and subsequently building the walls to the rim by adding coils of clay. The juncture of the coils is smoothed by the paddle-and-anvil technique. The potter holds a flat stone "anvil" inside the vessel and slaps against it from the outside with a wooden paddle curved to fit the desired contour. In the 1950s we listened as a middle-aged woman told us that as a little girl growing up in the village of Coyote Sits (Ban Dak) she used to awaken early on a summer morning to the wonderful sound of the slap-slap-slap of paddles hitting the clay on pots being made in nearly every yard. In 1958 there was one potter in Coyote Sits. Now there are none. And throughout the Papago country there are probably fewer than a dozen, including Laura Kermen, Laura Antone of Poso Verde, and María Domínguez of Many Dogs.

Papago pottery is a metaphor for Papago history and culture. It was once a utility product, a convenient class of objects that could be made with locally available materials. Every piece that was fired was intended for use by Papagos in cooking, storage, carrying, serving, or ceremony. In time, however, especially during the second half of the nineteenth century, Papagos were inexorably drawn into the cash economy of a more powerful people who came as foreigners to the desert. Metal utensils, bought with money, began to replace less durable Papago ceramics. Pottery began increasingly to be made for cash sale, and more and more the forms and decorations on pottery became a response to the market demands of non-Indians. Potters began to turn out flower pots, mugs, pencil holders, umbrella stands, and tiny painted vessels whose only purpose was decorative. The process has continued to the present in a downward spiral. Papago pottery lacks the glamor of highly polished and finely decorated wares made by the Southwest's Pueblo Indians; it is regarded by collectors as too crude. Given the comparatively small amount of money a potter can earn from selling her wares, most Papago women can spend their time more profitably in other ways. What is surprising is not the disappearance of Papago pottery as a viable craft. What is surprising is that there are any women who make it at all today.

Among the pieces in my own collection of Papago pottery is another metaphor. It is a figurine, a six-inch-high bird modelled out of white clay and decorated with a little red paint. On the top of the bird's head are eight small holes. The woman who made the vessel clearly intended it to be a saltshaker. It would serve the purpose admirably were it not for one major problem: there is no opening into which to put the salt! That is, not unless one had the patience of Job and were willing to fill the shaker through the top, one grain of salt at a time.

This pottery saltshaker came from the western side of the Papago Reservation—not far from Ajo, Arizona, where it was purchased in a store. The woman who made it doubtless had seen saltshakers in stores and restaurants and perceived they were objects white people used. My speculation is that her own experience with salt had not been with the packaged, iodized kind one buys in a supermarket, but rather with the coarse-grained Mexican variety. This is salt with large crystals that is kept in a bowl on the table to be dispensed with fingers or a spoon.

Be that as it may, it is clear the creator of this unique saltshaker had never had to fill one. What she did was copy the outward, visible form of a saltshaker in a native material, something that would look "Indian" to a potential buyer. Her sole purpose in making it was to sell it. Bird effigy saltshakers are not a Papago household utensil.

Thus it is over the whole range of cross-cultural perceptions. What Papagos see of us, just as what we see of them, are *forms*, the outward and readily perceivable shapes of things. What we cannot see, much less understand, are the subtle meanings members of a particular society attach to the forms of that society. And if the meanings are not shared between members of different cultures, the uses and functions of its forms become frightfully skewed, like images in a badly shattered mirror. It is true not only for saltshakers; it is true for all of a society's institutions. We might recognize, for example, that a Papago household consists of a mother, father, children of differing ages and sexes, uncles, aunts, and grandparents, but we cannot understand how that household functions unless we know what Papagos consider to be appropriate behaviors for "mother," "father," "uncle," "aunt," "elder brother," et cetera. What is sure is that the expected behaviors, like the kinship terms themselves, are not identical to those in societies other than Papago.

So we go about together, Papagos and the rest of us, seeing one another but not understanding. Each of us attributes to the other his own motives, values, beliefs, and ideals. Historically, the result of this kind of superficial interaction has been the Never Land that exists on American Indian reservations, the Papago Reservation included. To set foot on an Indian reservation is to risk falling with Alice down the rabbit hole. What would strike one as being bizarre or absurd anywhere else in the world seems acceptable on a reservation. Even commonplace. It is Wonderland and Through the Looking Glass, both volumes in one.

The Papago Reservation is in many ways a graveyard of good intentions, an enclosure of mutual misunderstandings. The all too pervasive habitual drunkenness, violence, suicide, incarceration, and economic dependency among the reservation's Indian people are not there because anyone wanted it that way. They are partially the result of terrible mistakes made by people who have been well meaning: federal bureaucrats, school teachers, missionaries, and others whose job it has been to "improve" the lot of Papagos. They are also the product of the Papagos' own miscalculations concerning their long-range interests. Time and again Papagos have traded away self-respect that comes with economic and social independence, sacrificing control of family and community affairs for short-term gains. Too frequently they have relinquished their right to make significant decisions in their own behalf. Rather than formulating their own plans and setting their own goals, Papagos often find themselves in the position of having to respond with a "yes" or "no" to plans formulated in their behalf. These involve health care, housing, community food programs, educational programs, and economic development. When individuals or communities can no longer devise and carry out their own schemes

*A bull is the winner at the Chuichu
championship junior rodeo, Arizona*

Interlude at the Chuichu rodeo

Calf roping at the Chuichu rodeo

Spectators at the Chuichu rodeo

for acomplishment, the collective psychological and socio-logical impacts are devastating.

No one knows precisely how many Papagos live in the United States. Estimates are that at any given moment from 6,000 to 7,000 people live on the combined areas of the Papago Reservation, with again that many Papagos living in such off-reservation communities as Phoenix, Tucson, Ajo, Casa Grande, Eloy, Marana, South Tucson, Stanfield, and elsewhere in Arizona. Others reside in Los Angeles, San Jose, and Oakland, California; still more live in such faraway places as Chicago and Cleveland.

The main Papago Reservation shares a sixty-four-mile border with Sonora, from where it goes north to within ten miles of Casa Grande. It takes in most of the acreage between Tucson and Ajo, 2,774,370 acres, to be exact. The San Xavier Reservation encompasses 71,095 acres; the Gila Bend Reservation has shrunk to 10,409 acres since it was established in 1882. In 1974 a 20-acre Papago settlement at Florence, Arizona, was added to the reserva-tion, making a grand total of 2,855,894 acres or 4,462 square miles. Not only does this make the Papago Reser-vation the second largest in the United States in terms of land area, with the Navajo Reservation ranking number one, but it also means Papagos own about four percent of all the land in Arizona. It is actually land held in trust for Papagos by the federal government, with the Bureau of Indian Affairs (BIA) within the Department of the Interior playing the role of on-the-ground trustee.

About 150 locations on the Papago Reservation have been mapped as settlements. Of these, about a third con-tinue to be occupied. The major communities, with popu-lations greater than one hundred, are those of Sells, the tribal capital and headquarters for the reservation's federal agencies; San Xavier, famous for its Spanish colonial period Franciscan mission; Gu Achi (Santa Rosa); Little Tucson; Hickiwan; Gu Oidak (Big Fields); Gu Wo (Kerwo); Topawa; Chuichu; Pisinimo; and Covered Wells (Quijotoa). All the people on the Gila Bend Reservation, nearly three hundred of them, live in San Lucy village.

*Lead singer of Just Us performing at the Chuichu
championship junior rodeo, Arizona*

Other settlements, with names like San Pedro, Sil Nakya, Cababi, Havana Nakya, Ali Chuk (Menager's Dam), Kaka, Charco 27, Coyote Sits, Santa Lucia, Queens Well, Cold Fields, Kohatk, and North Komelik, must be described as small. Some are only two- or three-household communities.

The "Papago Tribe of Arizona" is a white man's invention. Early in the twentieth century there were two major attempts to mold disparate Papago dialect and groups of related villages into a single whole. Fomented by non-Papagos, these efforts resulted in the competing League of Papago Chiefs and the Good Government League. Neither enjoyed federally sanctioned status, with the result that federal agents, rather than Papagos, obtained and maintained control of reservation-wide affairs. Traditional local control in the villages, however, remained strong.

In 1934 Congress passed the Indian Reorganization Act, a law that allowed Indians living on reservations throughout the United States to organize themselves under federally approved constitutions and by-laws. In 1937 the Papagos adopted a tribal constitution and by-laws, and the Papago Tribe of Arizona came into being. Following the lines of grazing districts that had been created in 1935, eleven political districts were created: nine on the main reservation and one each for San Xavier and Gila Bend.

Today, each district elects two councilmen to represent it on the tribal council; the chairman, vice-chairman, secretary, and treasurer are elected at large. The twenty-two-member tribal council meets at least once a month at Sells to pass tribal ordinances and resolutions and to pass judgment on various kinds of proposed contracts between the tribe and outsiders. Neither the state of Arizona nor local counties have legal jurisdiction on the reservation except in instances specifically approved by the tribe or provided for in federal law. Federal laws, of course, do apply on the reservation. Crimes involving counterfeiting, smuggling, and those relating to the mails are under the jurisdiction of federal courts as are major crimes such as murder, rape, arson, burglary, larceny, incest, and embezzlement of tribal funds. Otherwise, offenses committed on the reservation are defined by tribal ordinances and are tried in tribal court.

Institutions such as tribal councils, voting, representative government, tribal courts, district governments, written ordinances and resolutions, and officials such as a chairman operating at a "tribal" level were completely alien to Papago culture until the twentieth century. Government at the village level was presided over by a headman who earned the post because of his character and personality, and community decisions were made on the basis of consensus among all adult males. Adult females wielded their power in the household.

Village meetings were, by definition, among relatives, friends, and neighbors. They were democratic in the extreme, not unlike old-fashioned New England town hall meetings. No one "represented" anyone other than one's self in such meetings; all voices were heard and respected.

When the first elected "representatives" were sent to Sells to hold meetings to consider affairs for the entire reservation, they behaved in the only way they knew how. The protocol for village meetings was simply transplanted to Sells. Decisions still involved consensus, and "representatives" made their decisions based on the context of the Sells meeting rather than on any abstract consideration of what the "constituents" at home would or would not like. In other words, for many years the tribal council meetings were conducted as if they were village meetings. Representative government as citizens of the United States understand it was another saltshaker that had been handed the Papagos. They copied the form, but no one told them a way must be provided to get the salt in.

Although during the 1970s Papago councilmen began to split their votes on various measures and to behave increasingly in ways a non-Indian politician would understand, many Papagos still feel uncomfortable in the role of representative. Most Papagos, it appears, while striving for cooperation with one's fellows, remain strongly individualistic. It is enough that one should know oneself and to be one's own person. To try to know what is in the head and heart of another person, and thereby to be in a position to represent that person's views, is presumptuous in the extreme.

Between village government, with its town hall democracy, and tribal government, with its decision-making committees and its representational republicanism, there is a large warp that few of the participants comprehend. Ancient Papago tradition, born in the setting of rural desert communities, covertly survives in the modern guise of a constitution and by-laws born in English common law.

What makes the situation with respect to Papago tribal government all the more interesting is that the tribal government has become the principal dispenser of income on the reservation. Cattle raising is the largest productive industry, but eighty percent of the cattle are owned by fewer than twenty percent of the tribal members. Copper mines on the reservation in the Sif Oidak and San Xavier districts employ a few Papagos, and leasing and royalty monies go to those districts and to the tribe. At San Xavier, allottees who have lands in the mining area receive individual payments as well.

Beyond copper and cattle, however, and discounting an unknown amount of income earned by women who make and sell baskets, money on the reservation comes from tribal and federal sources. There is a cooperative farm at San Xavier, but its profits are small and its beneficiaries are largely those Papagos living at San Xavier.

The Bureau of Indian Affairs and the Indian Health Service, which operates a hospital at Sells and clinics at Santa Rosa and San Xavier, employ Papagos. The Indian Oasis School District, with elementary schools at Sells and Topawa and a high school in Sells, is another employer of Papagos. The Bureau of Indian Affairs operates elementary schools at San Simon, Santa Rosa, and Santa Rosa Ranch. There is also a parochial school at San Xavier staffed by Franciscan sisters.

It is the tribe itself, though, that administers a bewildering array of its own and federal funds for projects relating to housing, health care, preschools, senior citizens, alcohol addiction, and much, much more. The tribe has its own utility authority and is responsible for electric service to most parts of the main reservation. There is a tribal herd; there are range improvement programs; there are programs to develop new sources of water for cattle and crops. All of these services require large numbers of people to provide them; most of the providers are themselves Papagos. If federal funds were curtailed drastically, the results would be disastrous.

The Bureau of Indian Affairs has paved a fairly elaborate network of roads throughout the reservation. This makes it easier to bus children long distances to attend day schools. It also makes it easier for village residents to get from one place to another. There are plenty of cars and pickup trucks on the reservation; at least someone in nearly every extended family, although not in every household, is likely to own a car or truck. Otherwise, there are people such as Community Health Representatives employed by the tribe who live in the larger villages and who have sedans or vans available to transport people. Wagons, common even as recently as the mid-1950s, are now antiques. And except for Papago cowboys and people who ride for pleasure, hardly anyone uses horses for transportation today. The only people who walk are those unsuccessful in hitching a ride. Like wagons, they are rare as a means of transportation.

Beneath this heavy veneer of modernity, Papago traditional culture is alive, if not altogether well. Dozens of illustrations could be cited, but perhaps the best one—paradoxically enough—concerns Papago churches.

Every Arizona Papago "village" worthy of the name has a church or chapel. There are between sixty-five and seventy such structures on or immediately adjacent to the reservation, some of them in villages long abandoned. The anthropologist James Griffith, who has made a careful study of churches among Papago Indians, pointed out there are essentially three kinds of chapels: (1) those built by Franciscans, Roman Catholic churches intended for the indoor administration of the sacraments of the Roman

Catholic church; (2) those built by Papagos but with heavy influence from Franciscan missionaries; and (3) chapels built by Papagos with little or no help or encouragement from Franciscans. There are also Protestant churches, chiefly in Sells, since an estimated ten percent of Papagos are Protestant. The remainder are at least nominally Roman Catholic.

According to Griffith, chapels built without the benefit of clergy:

> ... provide the setting for the rituals and ceremonies of the folk Catholicism of the Papago Indians, or "Sonora Catholicism," as it is often called. This ... tradition of Catholicism probably came to Papagos in the second half of the 19th century, and was learned by them in northern Sonora. While Roman Catholic ritual involves the administration of the sacraments by full time religious specialists [i.e., priests], "Sonora Catholic" ritual is more concerned with the collection of sacred images, the community recitation of sacred texts, and community participation in regularly scheduled feasts. Sonora chapels provide a setting for the activities.

By "the setting" Griffith means more than the chapel alone. The chapel is part of a larger complex, one which includes a dance floor in front of the church; a row or two of wooden benches next to the dance floor; an enclosure parallel to one side of the dance floor where Papago musicians sit while playing dance music; a field cross, or *cruz mayor*, at a considerable distance from the portal of the church, usually facing it; and a nearby feast house and cooking area beneath a ramada where food is cooked and where those attending the feast can sit down—in shifts—to a meal of beans, chili con carne, salad, iced tea or Kool-Aid, wheat flour tortillas, wheat buns, and frosted cake for dessert.

One characteristic of Papago-built chapels is that they

The cruz mayor *(field cross), Santa Cruz village
(Koson Vaya, or Wood Rat Well), Arizona*

St. Elizabeth's chapel, Vaiva Vo (Cocklebur), Arizona

are small, sometimes even tiny. Part of the reason is because the widths of such buildings depend on the lengths of locally available roofing beams. An even more important reason, however, is that the important function of a chapel is to house religious artifacts, such as the holy images brought from Magdalena, and to provide enough space so a few people can sit down to recite the rosary or otherwise pray in the presence of those artifacts. Most traditional ritual, including processions, dancing, and the preparation of a feast, takes place outdoors. The sacred area of Papago chapels is more than the floor space inside. It includes a much larger area in front where most public display of religious devotion actually occurs. The dances may appear to be secular in that they consist mainly of polkas, waltzes, and schottisches played in their own style by Papago dance bands. They are, however, an integral part of religious celebrations.

It is tempting to speculate, as James Griffith has done, that the Papago notion of religious space as being essentially an outdoor area, with religious structures intended for comparatively private devotions and as sanctuaries for sacred objects, is a cultural survival reflecting the Papagos' Aztec roots. Among the civilizations of Mesoamerica, religious architecture—as monumental as it was—was designed to house religious relics rather than to accommodate public rituals under roof. Public ceremonies took place on top of or outside of Aztec temples, not in them. Is such a shared notion purely accidental?

Franciscan-built churches in Papago country reflect a wholly different notion of religious space. With Mission San Xavier del Bac leading the list, they are uniformly larger. They are built to accommodate public religious ritual indoors. Not only are religious objects kept in Franciscan churches, but what are considered to be the important parts of religious ceremonies are conducted in them for entire congregations. The sacred area, the sanctuary, is thought of by non-Papagos as being inside the church rather than outdoors.

The rain house at Gu Oidak (Big Fields), Arizona

In a few Franciscan-built churches the villagers have seized at least partial control of the space, converting it— however unconsciously—into a form with which they are more at ease. They have taken side altars, baptistries, or sacristies for their own, adorning them and sheets hung as retables with their holy images from Magdalena. Let the missionary have the main altar if he wants it! At San Xavier del Bac, overwhelmed by thousands of tourists and many hundreds of non-Papagos who attend church services there, the local people have retreated to the village feast house for their more traditional Catholic devotions where they recite prayers and sing hymns in Spanish. Their images of saints are kept in private homes.

The most important surviving aboriginal Papago religious ritual in Arizona is the annual saguaro wine feast, or *nawait i'ita* (wine drinks), as Papagos say. It continues to be held each year in two or three villages on the main reservation, and in 1980 the people at Pisinimo, in a minicultural revival, were building a round house in which to ferment the wine.

The round house and a ramada in front of it are the only structures associated with this feast, the purpose of which is to bring rain to the desert. The ceremony is one that involves ritual speeches (prayers), eating, drinking wine fermented from saguaro fruit, singing, and dancing to the accompaniment of native musical instruments. Not surprisingly, these same elements: song, dance, prayer, feasting, drinking, and music—but in wholly different guises—are essential in the rituals surrounding "Sonora Catholicism." It is also not surprising that the round house is where religious paraphernalia are temporarily stored and where the more private parts of the *nawait i'ita*, such as the fermentation of the wine, occur. One has only to look at a round house and at a Papago chapel to see that the latter is an accommodation of the former. Papagos in Christian garb still carry the secret of the O'odham way within them. They are more cosmopolitan and far more tolerant than most of the rest of us.

Altar in the chapel at Santa Lucia (Gu Wo, or Wildcat), Arizona

*Sanctuary of St. Anthony's Church, Supi Oidak
(Cold Fields), Arizona*

Statue of Santa Clara (Saint Clair of Assisi) in the Church of the Sacred Heart, Comobabi, Arizona

Cross on the chapel at Santa Cruz village (Koson Vaya, or Wood Rat Well), Arizona

It took Papagos a long time to hammer introduced forms of Christianity into shapes they could cope with. How well they will manage with the heightened onrush of the outside world, now delivered via paved roads, radio, and television, only time will tell. The reservation is everywhere littered with the physical evidence of Papagos being set upon by the white man and of Papagos being unable to digest the offerings. Some areas of Papago residence are littered with tin cans, aluminum cans, empty bottles, disposable diapers, and empty cartons of Colonel Sanders Kentucky Fried Chicken. Some Papago yards are cemeteries of dead automobiles and pickup trucks.

Then there is larger litter. There are abandoned mines and their attendant debris; there are active mines that one day will leave as their only legacy enormous holes in the desert. The Tat Momolikot Dam, the sixth largest earthen dam in the world, stretches two and a half miles over Santa Rosa Wash. It was built between 1972 and 1974 by the U.S. Army Corps of Engineers at a cost of $10,000,000. It is designed to check a possible once-in-a-hundred-years flash flood. In the meantime, "Lake St. Clair" behind the dam is a catchment of blowing tumbleweeds. The promised tourists, water-skiers, and fishermen—like the water itself—never materialized. South of Pisinimo there are about three thousand acres of cleared farm land, deep wells, and concrete-lined irrigation ditches, an effort at industrial farming that began in 1958. Since then, Papago Farms, as it is called, has been an on-again off-again proposition, frequently abandoned in the face of litigation and acrimonious controversy.

Among the many abandoned mines on the Papago Reservation is one on the far western side known as the Gunsight. Patented in the 1870s by non-Indians, the mining claim is said to have yielded $80,000 in silver before it closed down early in this century. Gunsight is also said to have gotten its name from a hammered silver sight on a rifle—whether an Indian's or a white man's is in dispute—with the silver having come from the place where the mine was subsequently developed.

Lake St. Clair behind Tat Momolikot Dam in Arizona

When the Gunsight was still in operation, an entrepreneur named William Haynes (or Haines) dug a 125-foot deep well and started a small goat ranch a mile north of the mine. In 1915 he sold the well and ranch to John Blair, who switched livestock from goats to cattle. He also planted ten acres of corn, sorghum, and milo maize. Sometime after January 1928, Ben J. McKinney bought the 320-acre Blair Ranch. He bought poultry and added three large chicken houses roofed with galvanized iron.

In 1931 the federal government bought all of Mr. McKinney's holdings in the Papago country, including the Blair Ranch, and added them to the reservation. Juan Luis, a Papago from Pozo Redondo, about eight miles to the north, took possession of the ranch that Papagos had come to call Schuchulik, or "Place of the Chickens." Juan Luis's relatives moved to be near him. Among them were Flora and Carlos Santos, his sister and brother-in-law. In 1939 Flora decided she wanted a chapel. Carlos put up the money to hire a Papago stonemason and Papago carpenter. The local men pitched in as laborers with women preparing their meals. On April 4, 1940, Father Regis Rohder dedicated the church. He named it St. Martin in honor of the Franciscan Father Provincial at the time who had donated the bell for the chapel. From the completion of this small stone chapel to the present, Gunsight, or Chickens, or Schuchulik—take your choice—has been a permanent Papago village.

In 1978 the National Aeronautics and Space Administration (NASA) built an experimental photovoltaic system for generating electrical power in Schuchulik. The cost was somewhere between $300,000 and $400,000. On a hot July day in 1979, John Schaefer and I drove to Schuchulik to see for ourselves. On the way we picked up an elderly man walking westward along the shoulder of State Highway 86. He had been in Sells; he was headed for his home in Schuchulik, fifty-five miles away. With typical Papago nonchalance, he was totally unsurprised to find out we were going to his home village. It was almost as if he had been expecting us. But it was good luck for John and me. When we told him we were interested in the solar generator, he told us to see David Santos and pointed out his house. Not that finding anyone in Schuchulik is a difficult task. It is not a very big place. At the time of our visit there were about twenty houses, including one or two large mobile homes; some houses built as part of a federal project and whose building materials and appearances were thoroughly non-Papago; some stone houses; and some adobe houses. We learned there were sixteen households. Three or four groups of householders were away, though, members of those families working in various kinds of off-reservation employment.

St. Martin's church, a typical "Sonora Catholic" chapel, was there with its full complement of dance floor, bandstand, feast house, cooking area, and field cross. It was obvious that Schuchulik was a member in good standing of the reservation's network of fiestas that are now generally held on weekends to accommodate school and employment schedules. Schuchulik routinely celebrates a fiesta in honor of St. Francis in May—their own unique date for that event—and one for St. Martin, Bishop of Tours, in November. These are in addition to processionless fiestas held on the occasion of a baptism, wedding, birthday, graduation, or first communion. Papagos know how to give a party, and at such a time as many as five hundred people might be expected to visit Schuchulik to dance to polka or waltz music and to enjoy free food. Someone else has pointed out that on fiesta day a village becomes a huge restaurant with all comers taking part in a feast.

David Santos, village headman and Keeper of the Photovoltaic Cell System, was home. He cheerily dropped whatever it was he had been doing to give the two of us a tour of the new facilities. These included the cement block "domestic services building" that contained a washing machine, with hot water courtesy of a solar collector on its roof; a sewing machine; and fifteen (for sixteen households) 4.7-cubic-foot refrigerators, each with a small freezing compartment. Five compressors ran all fifteen refrigerators in units of three each.

Here, in the church, and in houses throughout the village, were forty-seven fluorescent lamps equipped with twenty-watt elements. And most important of all, there was a two-horsepower electric motor that ran a water pump capable of delivering 1,100 gallons per hour into the village water distribution system.

All of these appliances operated on direct current rather than standard alternating current. This meant lamps, sewing machine, washing machine, and motor had to be specially built. None of the appliances would run on alternating current supplied to most homes elsewhere on the reservation by the Papago Tribal Utility Authority.

The electricity generated to run these utilities came from twenty-four solar-cell panels arranged in three long rows. They are collectively referred to by NASA as a "photovoltaic array." These silent, gleaming devices look wonderfully out of place in the Sonoran Desert, even more so by Schuchulik's mesquite corral. Were it not for the more homely chain link fence surrounding the panels, one might think they had been left there by a Martian.

The beaming down of the sun's rays into the panels generates the 120-volt direct current. From the panels it goes into a control room crammed with meters, graphs, and gauges as well as with a bank of fifty-three lead-calcium batteries connected in series.

We asked David Santos, who is the volunteer caretaker of all this equipment, and who regularly takes readings from the instruments and sends reports to NASA, what happens when something breaks down. One of the compressors operating three refrigerators was not working when we were there, for example, and neither was the panel box controlling the automatic timer on the hot water heater.

"I call Cleveland," was the answer.

"Cleveland, Ohio?"

"Yes."

Cleveland, Ohio, is home for the Lewis Research Center of the National Aeronautics and Space Administration. It was here that the system was designed. It is here that responsibility for maintaining the system rests.

"Will somebody come all the way from Cleveland to fix the compressor?"

"Oh, no. I'll tell Cleveland what's wrong and they will call somebody in Phoenix or Tucson to come fix it."

To telephone, Santos had to leave the village. There are no phones in Schuchulik. But in the real world, he works for the San Simon School, some twenty miles to the east. Maybe he used a phone at the school. Or he could go to Why, Arizona, a mere five miles away, and use a phone there.

Before 1978, there were four small, gasoline-powered electrical generators in Schuchulik. When in working condition, they powered—and still do—a few television sets, electric irons, stereos, and blenders for grinding red chili. The small amount of power generated by NASA's system would be insufficient to supply the needs of a single medium-size all-electrical home, one with wall receptacles and appliances for heating, cooling, and cooking. Moreover, the Lewis Center has estimated the cost of Schuchulik's electricity at $1.76 per kilowatt hour. Residents of Tucson, Arizona, pay 6.5 cents per kilowatt hour.

For David Santos, it seemed to us, the centerpiece of the village's new system was the water pump and the tiny motor that ensured a reliable flow of water. Indeed, the story of the pump is the story of why Schuchulik became "the world's first solar village."

The old pump, Santos explained, was powered by a diesel engine. As the engine grew in age and use, it became balkier. In time, he was the only person in the village who understood its idiosyncracies well enough to be able to start it consistently.

Then the day came that Santos decided to visit Los Angeles for a week. He instructed some boys in the operation of the diesel engine, then left on his trip. The boys could not make the engine run. Schuchulik spent a week without water. Given the trauma of that experience in the lives of some sixty-five people, it is not surprising that they were ready to listen when NASA engineers proposed a system that would keep their water flowing. Electric lights to replace kerosene lanterns; refrigerators in which to keep medicines (like many Papagos, the people of Schuchulik have a high incidence of diabetes and must take insulin); a wringer washing machine; and a sewing machine—these were just icing on the cake. It is water that really matters.

So the big pump powered by a tiny motor does its job. The pump, painted bright orange, and the electric motor are surrounded by a chain link fence. The enclosed area is perhaps fifty square feet. Santos pointed with pride to the fine crop of acorn squash he had growing inside the fence. He said cottontails could wriggle underneath, but it didn't matter. There would be plenty of squash for cottontails and people alike. His ancestors would have understood.

Before we left Schuchulik, our genial guide showed us business cards of recent visitors. What was once the place of many chickens had been descended upon by executives, engineers, government officials, journalists, and captains of industry from all over the world: Japan, South America, Africa, and even Russia.

More important, though, was the fact that some relatives from Los Angeles had arrived in Schuchulik two days before our visit.

"We were sitting around talking," Santos said, " and we got to talking about rabbits. My sister said it had been a long time since she had eaten one. She remembered how good they are. So yesterday evening I drove to Wall's Well. There are always a lot of rabbits there. I shot two, and we ate them last night. It was sure good, and those people liked it."

David Santos's ancestors would have understood that, also. And they would have approved with all their hearts.

Danny

Big Fields, or Gu Oidak, is a "conservative" Papago village. But while standing next to the field cross opposite the front of the local chapel, one listens in vain to hear Papago being spoken. The children playing in nearby yards are speaking only English.

Papago songs of twenty-five years ago have given way to the sounds of rock and roll and disco music pouring out of countless radios turned up full volume. The soft yellow glow of kerosene lanterns has been replaced by the eerie blue of television picture tubes.

Were it not for federal intervention, dozens of small

Danny Lopez

Papago settlements would long ago have been abandoned, their residents gone to off-reservation cities and towns to make their way in the urban world. As it is, many villages are kept in operation only because of funds coming from such sources as the Tribal Work Experience Program (TWEP), the Youth Program under the Comprehensive Employment Training Act (CETA), Community Health Representative (CHR) program, social security, pensions, and short-term government jobs. These are supplemented by programs involving food stamps, food commodities, and food vouchers. Houses are built with government funds; wells are drilled and water and sanitation systems are installed courtesy of the Indian Health Service. Roads are constructed and paved by the Bureau of Indian Affairs. Knowing how to survive in the Sonoran Desert has come to mean knowing how to get public funds. It is not a very productive way of life, and for many of the participants it is a depressing and debilitating one.

But if farming as a viable means of subsistence has all but stopped, fiestas have not. If the "native" religion continues to be savored by only a few and to be preserved chiefly in printed form, the Papagos' own brand of Roman Catholicism, and even of Protestantism, has comfortably taken its place. If the serious business of raising cattle for profit now rests in the hands of a small number of families, the love of horses and of "cowboy culture" remains widespread. Rodeos rank with baseball games as being among the most popular sports on the reservation.

If the rest of the world has determined that the proper destiny of Papagos is assimilation, Papagos seem just as determined to remain as "Papagos," however much the meaning of that concept may change through time.

If my friend Antonio Reyes embodied the essence of the recent Papago past, it may be that my friend Danny Lopez has within him a hint of the Papago future.

Together, we visited Gu Oidak. Before this, we had stood together on the summit of Baboquivari Peak, the physical and spiritual center of the Papago universe. So had we stood on the roof of Mission San Ignacio, on a hundreds-of-years-old trail west of Sil Nakya, and at the edge of the pond at Quitovac. Now, however, we were home. Not my home, but Danny's home.

Growing near the house where his parents live in Gu Oidak is a mesquite tree. He pointed to a spot on the ground beneath the tree. "That," he said, "is where I was born."

I marvelled. How many of us, I thought to myself, can point to a place on the earth and say with honesty it marks the location where we first emerged into sunlight or starlight? Here was where Danny first breathed the desert air; this is where he uttered his first cries as a human being. Not twenty miles away "somewhere," not even a mile away nor ten feet to the left or right. But here. On this very spot!

Emergence for most of us is a hospital happening, an event surrounded by medical paraphernalia and the studied indifference of our medical subculture. Hospitals, like their personnel, come and go. Small wonder that we lack a sense of place, of roots. We are born in Rochester or Phoenix or Denver or New Orleans. But Danny was not born in Gu Oidak. He was born *there*, under that mesquite tree on that piece of ground. Roots and a sense of place? How could it be otherwise?

We walked to the round house where in times gone by the saguaro fruit juice had been fermented into rain-bringing wine. For a place so little used in recent years it was in good condition. Danny recalled there used to be homes much closer to the round house than now. And he remembered the crowds who used to come to wager on foot races between the men of Gu Oidak and of some neighboring village. We moved the door of the round house to one side, stooped close to the earth, and entered this aboriginal Papago chapel. We lingered awhile, stooped low once more, and straightened up in the sunshine. Danny carefully replaced the brush door before we left.

With Danny's father, a handsome man with legs bowed from years in the saddle, we drove to Koson Vaya (Wood Rat Well). Resting inconspicuously on the west face of the

Clara Lopez, Gu Oidak (Big Fields), Arizona

*Ramon Lopez, Danny Lopez's father, at Santa Cruz village
(Koson Vaya, or Wood Rat Well), Arizona*

South Comobabi Mountains, this settlement a generation earlier had been one of the winter or well villages of the summer *temporal* of Gu Oidak. Danny's parents and grandparents had lived here, some of them working sporadically in nearby but now long-abandoned mines. With three dug wells and reliable water, Koson Vaya had resisted being altogether forgotten when the mines closed. Cattlemen took it over. A chapel was built—complete with bandstand, field cross, dance floor, feast house, and cooking ramada—and dedicated to Santa Cruz.

Now, however, the last resident was an old man. He was hospitalized. Speculation was that he would never return unless it would be to the cemetery across the arroyo. Relatives living in Nolia, a village on the flats below and to the west, looked after the structures, including the chapel complex and two or three still-standing and roofed houses. Their branded Herefords roamed freely over the hills.

Danny's father took him on a walking tour of the ruins of Koson Vaya. He pointed to stone footings among the cactus where houses had once stood, telling Danny this relative or that relative had once lived there. Danny learned many things about his family's history he had never known. I followed along behind father and son, listening in awe. It was a living history tour of an archaeological site. The house locations, the wells, the trails largely overgrown with desert vegetation, and even the pieces of broken earthenware and ironstone pottery came alive. A two-dimensional ruin became a three-dimensional panorama in the animated memory and conversation of Danny's father.

We drove back to Gu Oidak. Danny's mother was in the enclosed yard of her house seated on a chair weaving a large basket out of yucca, beargrass, and devil's claw. We were introduced to her. Danny explained she knew no English, only Papago. His father could speak quite a bit of English.

We were invited into the house for coffee and a little something to eat. The conversation was quiet, warm, and

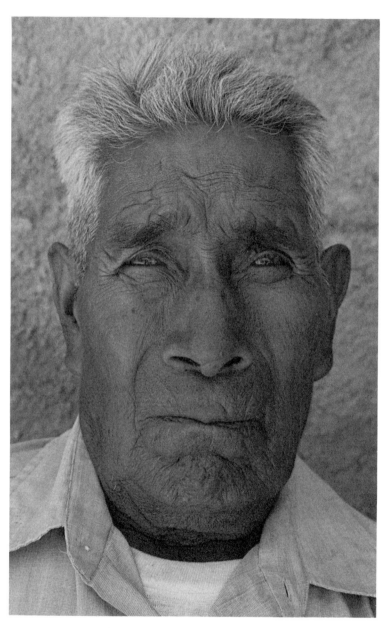

Juan Lopez, San Luis village, Arizona

pleasant. Danny's mother and father were two people who clearly loved and respected one another. They knew who they were. They were as solid and as secure as the beautiful desert that had surrounded them all of their lives. I told Danny he was fortunate to have such parents. He agreed.

Danny Lopez had not spent his whole life in Gu Oidak. At an early age he had gone away to school, and at a time when it was still forbidden for Indian children to speak their native language in the classroom or on the playground. They were punished if caught doing so. In Danny's case, this was a Catholic boarding school run by Franciscans.

So in ways subtle and ways not so subtle, he grew to maturity being taught that it was somehow "bad" to be a Papago. If it was wrong to speak one's language, it was also wrong to be oneself. Gu Oidak, with its dirt-floored adobe houses, had to be a "backward" place. And what about a mother who could speak only Papago?

As a young man, Danny got into his share of trouble, some of that trouble involving liquor. In time, he married and had children of his own. He moved to Tucson and got a job working in a copper mine south of the city. But reaching toward middle age, he began to realize what had happened to him, as well as to hundreds of other Papagos, during his youth. He came to perceive that white men had tried to alienate him from his familial and cultural roots. And he decided to do something about it.

He worked with friends and relatives to organize the Desert Indian Dancers, a group of Papago children who, with the help of elders, began to learn the old Papago songs and native dances. He quit his job in the mine and took a lower paying and less secure position working for the Indian Oasis School District in Sells. He worked especially with the younger pupils, taking them on field trips to Papago shrines and to other places of historical and cultural interest.

And so he continues to work with youth on the reservation and in Tucson, doing all in his power to let them know what is positive in the past, present, and future of

149

the Papago culture. He teaches Papagos to become literate in their own language. He has gone with the Desert Indian Dancers to performances in Washington, D.C.; Coronado National Memorial; and Tucson, lecturing to white audiences on Papago culture and chiding his audiences for their lack of sensitivity, knowledge, and tolerance.

Danny Lopez is a pragmatic dreamer. He knows the "old ways" are not going to return. But he also knows, as Henry David Thoreau knew, "The heavens stood over the heads of our ancestors as near as to us." What was good and just and right in their lives is equally so in ours, O'odham and white man alike. That is Danny's conviction. That we all come to understand this transcendent truth is the Papagos' hope.

Selected Bibliography

Anonymous

1856   [Carta: Real Presidio de San Pedro de la Conquista del Pitic en la Sonora, escribe Junio 24, 1744.] *Documentos para la Historia de México*, 3rd series, Vol. 4, pp. 675–82 México, D.F., Imprenta de Vicente García Torres.

Bahr, Donald M.

1973   "The Pima-Papago: Social Organization." Unpublished manuscript, copy on file with the author, Department of Anthropology, Arizona State University, Tempe.

BAHR, DONALD M.; JUAN GREGORIO, DAVID I. LOPEZ, and
ALBERT ALVAREZ

　1974　*Piman Shamanism and Staying Sickness (ká:cim múmkidag).* Tucson, The University of Arizona Press.

BLEVINS, WINFRED

　1979　"The World's First Solar Villagers Are Waiting to See." *Smithsonian,* Vol. 10, no. 8 (November), pp. 157–58, 160–67. Washington, D.C., Smithsonian Institution.

BOLTON, HERBERT E.

　1960　*Rim of Christendom. A Biography of Eusebio Francisco Kino, Pacific Coast Pioneer.* New York, Russell & Russell. [A reissue of the 1936 edition.]

BRINGAS DE MANZANEDA Y ENCINAS, DIEGO M.

　1977　*Friar Bringas Reports to the King: Methods of Indoctrination on the Frontier of New Spain, 1796–97.* Translated and edited by Daniel S. Matson and Bernard L. Fontana. Tucson, The University of Arizona Press.

BRYAN, KIRK

　1925　"The Papago Country, Arizona." *United States Geological Survey Water-Supply Paper,* no. 499. Washington, D.C., Government Printing Office.

CROSSWHITE, FRANK S.

　1980　"The Annual Saguaro Harvest and Crop Cycle of the Papago, with Reference to Ecology and Symbolism." *Desert Plants,* Vol. 2, no. 1 (Spring), pp. 2–61. Superior, Arizona, The University of Arizona for the Boyce Thompson Arboretum.

DAVIS, EDWARD H.

　1920　"The Papago Ceremony of Vikita." *Indian Notes and Monographs,* Vol. 3, no. 4, pp. 158–78. New York, Museum of the American Indian, Heye Foundation.

DENSMORE, FRANCES

1929 "Papago Music." *Bulletin of the Bureau of American Ethnology,* no. 90. Washington, D.C., Government Printing Office.

DOBYNS, HENRY F.

1960 "The Religious Festival." Unpublished Ph.D. dissertation, Cornell University, Ithaca, New York.

1972 "Military Transculturation of Northern Piman Indians, 1782–1821." *Ethnohistory,* Vol. 19, no. 4 (Fall), pp. 323–43. Tucson, American Society for Ethnohistory.

1972 *The Papago People.* Phoenix, Indian Tribal Series.

DOLAN, DARROW

1972 "The Plomo Papers." *Ethnohistory,* Vol. 19, no. 4 (Fall), pp. 305–22. Tucson, American Society for Ethnohistory.

FABILA, ALFONSO

1957 "Los Papagos de Sonora." *Acción Indigenista,* no. 47, pp. 2–4. México, D.F., Instituto Nacional Indigenista.

FONT, PEDRO

1975 "Letters of Friar Pedro Font, 1776–1777. Translated by Dan S. Matson. *Ethnohistory,* Vol. 22, no. 3 (Summer), pp. 263–93. Tucson, American Society for Ethnohistory.

FONTANA, BERNARD L.

1973 "The Cultural Dimensions of Pottery: Ceramics as Social Documents." In *Ceramics in America,* edited by Ian M. G. Quimby, pp. 1–13 [Winterthur Conference Report for 1972]. Charlottesville, University Press of Virginia.

1974 "Man in Arid Lands: the Piman Indians of the Sonoran Desert." In *Desert Biology,* Vol. 2, edited by George W. Brown, Jr., pp. 489–528. New York, Academic Press, Inc.

1976   "Meanwhile, Back at the Rancheria. . . ." *The Indian Historian*, Vol. 8, no. 4 (Winter), pp. 13–18. San Francisco, American Indian Historical Society.

1976   *The Papago Indians.* Three parts. Sells, Arizona, Title IV-A, Indian Education Act, Indian Oasis Schools.

FONTANA, BERNARD L.; WILLIAM J. ROBINSON, CHARLES W. CORMACK, and ERNEST E. LEAVITT, JR.

1962   *Papago Indian Pottery.* Seattle, University of Washington Press.

GRIFFITH, JAMES S.

1973   "The Catholic Religious Architecture of the Papago Reservation, Arizona." Unpublished Ph.D. dissertation, The University of Arizona, Tucson.

1974   "Franciscan Chapels on the Papagueria, 1912–1973." *Smoke Signal,* no. 30. Tucson, The Tucson Corral of the Westerners, Inc.

1975   "The Folk Chapels of the Papagueria." *Pioneer America*, Vol. 7, no. 2 (July), pp. 21–36. Falls Church, Virginia, The Pioneer America Society, Inc.

HASTINGS, JAMES R.

1959   "The Tragedy at Camp Grant in 1871." *Arizona and the West*, Vol. 1, no. 2 (Summer), pp. 146–60. Tucson, The University of Arizona Press.

IVES, RONALD L.

1965   "Population of the Pinacate Region, 1698–1706." *The Kiva*, Vol. 31, no. 1 (October), pp. 37–45. Tucson, Arizona Archaeological and Historical Society.

1966   "Kino's Exploration of the Pinacate Region." *The Journal of Arizona History*, Vol. 7, no. 2 (Summer), pp. 59–75. Tucson, Arizona Pioneers' Historical Society.

JOSEPH, ALICE; ROSAMUND B. SPICER, and JANE CHESKY

1949　*The Desert People: A Study of the Papago Indians.* Chicago, University of Chicago Press.

KILCREASE, A. T.

1939　"Ninety-five Years of History of the Papago Indians." *Southwestern Monuments Monthly Report,* supplement for April, pp. 297–310. Coolidge, Arizona, National Park Service.

KINO, EUSEBIO F.

1948　*Kino's Historical Memoir of Pimería Alta.* Translated and edited by Herbert E. Bolton. Two volumes in one. Berkeley and Los Angeles, University of California Press. [A reissue of the 1919 publication.]

1971　"Kino's Biography of Francisco Javier Saeta, S.J." Translated, with an epilogue, by Charles W. Polzer, S.J.; original Spanish text edited by Ernest J. Burrus, S.J. *Sources and Studies for the History of the Americas,* Vol. 9. Rome, Italy, and St. Louis, Missouri, Jesuit Historical Institute.

LAMBERTIE, CHARLES DE

1885　*Le drame de la Sonora, l'état de Sonora, M. le comte de Raousset-Boulbon et Charles de Pindray.* Paris, Chez Ledoyen, Libraire-Editeur.

LLOYD, JOHN W.

1911　*Aw-aw-tam Indian Nights.* Westfield, New Jersey, The Lloyd Group.

LUMHOLTZ, CARL

1971　*New Trails in Mexico.* Glorieta, New Mexico, The Rio Grande Press, Inc. [Reissue of the 1912 publication.]

McCARTY, KIERAN R., and DANIEL S. MATSON, *translators and editors*

n.d.　[A series of documents, dating 1826 through 1844, relating to Papago Indian-Mexican affairs of the period.] Original documents in the Archivo Historico del Estado de Sonora, Hermosillo, Sonora, Mexico. Unpublished translations and notes on file with Kieran McCarty, The University of Arizona Library, Tucson.

McGee, William J.

1894–   [The 1894–95 field diaries of W. J. McGee cover-
1895   ing his two expeditions into northwestern So-
        nora.] Unpublished field notebooks, on file in
        the Library of Congress, Washington, D.C.

Manje, Juan M.

1954   *Unknown Arizona and Sonora, 1693–1721.*
        Translated by Harry J. Karns. Tucson, Arizona
        Silhouettes.

Nolasco A., Margarita

1965   "Los Pápagos, habitantes del desierto." *Anales
        del Instituto Nacional Antropología e Historia,*
        Vol. 17, pp. 375–448. México, D.F., Secretaría de
        Educación Pública.

Pennington, Campbell W.

1980   *The Pima Bajo of Central Sonora, Mexico. Vol-
        ume 1. The Material Culture.* Salt Lake City,
        University of Utah Press.

Polzer, Charles W.

1972   *A Kino guide. His Missions—His Monuments.*
        3rd printing, revised. Tucson, Southwestern Mis-
        sion Research Center. [A revised and expanded
        version of the 1968 publication.]

Polzer, Charles W., *editor* and *translator*

1972   "The Franciscan Entrada into Sonora, 1645–1652.
        A Jesuit Chronicle." *Arizona and the West,* Vol.
        14, no. 3 (Autumn), pp. 253–78. Tucson, The
        University of Arizona Press.

SAXTON, DEAN, and LUCILLE SAXTON, *compilers* and
translators

1969 *Dictionary. Papago and Pima to English; English
to Papago and Pima.* Tucson, The University of
Arizona Press.

1973 *O'othham Hoho'ok A'Agitha; Legends and Lore
of the Papago and Pima Indians.* Tucson, The
University of Arizona Press.

SEDELMAYR, JACOBO

1939 "Sedelmayr's Relacion of 1746." Translated and
edited by Ronald L. Ives. *Bulletin of the Bureau
of American Ethnology,* no. 123, *Anthropological Papers,* no. 9, pp. 99–117. Washington, D.C.,
United States Government Printing Office.

STEWART, KENNETH M.

1965 "Southern Papago Salt Pilgrimages." *The Master-
key,* Vol. 39, no. 3 (July–September), pp. 84–91.
Los Angeles, Southwest Museum.

THACKERY, FRANK A., and A. R. LEDING

1929 "The Giant Cactus of Arizona; The Use of Its
Fruit and Other Cactus Fruits by the Indians."
Journal of Heredity, Vol. 20, no. 9 (September),
pp. 400–414. Baltimore, The American Genetic
Association.

UNDERHILL, RUTH M.

1938 "A Papago Calendar Record." *The University of
New Mexico Bulletin,* no. 322, *Anthropological
Series,* Vol. 2, no. 5 (March 1). Albuquerque, Uni-
versity of New Mexico.

1939 "Social Organization of the Papago Indians."
*Columbia University Contributions to Anthro-
pology,* Vol. 30. New York, Columbia University
Press.

1946 "Papago Indian Religion." *Columbia University*

Contributions to Anthropology, Vol. 33. New York, Columbia University Press.

1951   *People of the Crimson Evening.* Lawrence, Kansas, Bureau of Indian Affairs, Branch of Education, Haskell Institute.

1968   *Singing for Power. The Song Magic of the Papago Indians of Southern Arizona.* Berkeley and Los Angeles, University of California Press. [A reissue of the 1938 publication.]

1979   *The Papago and Pima Indians of Arizona.* Palmer Lake, Colorado, The Filter Press. [Reissue of *The Papago Indians of Arizona and their Relatives the Pima,* first published in 1940.]

1979   *Papago Woman.* New York, Holt, Rinehart, and Winston, Inc. [Reissue, with additional materials, of *The Autobiography of a Papago Woman,* published in 1936 as *Memoir* 46 of the American Anthropological Association.]

UNDERHILL, RUTH M.; DONALD M. BAHR; BAPTISTO LOPEZ; JOSE PANCHO; and DAVID LOPEZ

1979   "Rainhouse and Ocean. Speeches for the Papago Year." *American Tribal Religions,* Vol. 4. Flagstaff, Museum of Northern Arizona.

UNITED STATES CONGRESS. *Senate.*

1931   *Survey of Conditions of the Indians in the United States.* Hearings before a subcommittee of the Committee on Indian Affairs, United States Senate, 71st Congress, 3rd session. Part 17 (Arizona), pp. 7953–8899. Washington, D.C., United States Government Printing Office.

VELARDE, LUIS J.

1954   "This is the Description of the . . . Nations of the Pimería. . . ." In *Unknown Arizona and Sonora, 1693–1721,* by Juan M. Manje, translated by Harry J. Karns, pp. 221–67. Tucson, Arizona Silhouettes.

WADDELL, JACK O.

1973   *The Place of the Cactus Wine Ritual in the Papago Indian Ecosystem.* Chicago, IXth International Congress of Anthropological and Ethnological Sciences.

Index

Antropología, Mexico City, 93
Mututicachi, Sonora, 35

National Aeronautics and Space Administration (NASA), 136, 138–139
Navaho Indian Reservation, 75, 118
Niza, Marcos de, O.F.M., 36
Nogales, Arizona, 86
Nogales, Sonora, 107
Nolasco A., Margarita, 93
Noriego, Luciano, x, 102
North Komelik, Arizona, 120
Nuestra Señora de la Merced del Batki. *See* Batki, Arizona

Oacpicagigua, Luis, 62
Oblasser, Bonaventure, O.F.M., 76
Ocotillo, 14, 20
Officer, James E., x
O'odham, definition, xi. *Also see* Papago Indians, Pima Indians, and Piman Indians
O'odham *himdag. See* Papago Indians, religion
Opata Indians, 35, 53, 61
Oquitoa, Sonora, 89
Ortega, Margaret, x
Outing program. *See* Papago Indians, outing program

Pablo, Crispin, *pseud.*, 9
Papago Farms, 134
Papago Indian Reservation, 3, 90, 112–113, 118, 120; establishment, 75; roads, 123. *Also see* Papago Indians
Papago Indians, architecture, 48–49, 56, 57, 59, 87–88, 102, 123–124, 127, 129; basketry, 122, 147;

calendar, 11; calendar stick, 54, 69, 70, 73, 90; churches, 123–124, 127, 129; citizenship, 69; clothing, 59; criminal jurisdiction, 120–121; definition, 37–39; dialect groups, 47–48; disease, 50–51; economy, 49–50, 73–79, 86–88, 91, 122, 143; *ejidos,* 92; feasts, 129, 137; government, 59–60, 67–68, 96, 120–122; homeland, 11; in Mexico, 19–21, 30–31, 80–81, 83, 85–91, 96, 98–99, 102, 103–106, 109; Spanish influence on, 55–57, 59–63, 66, 67; land allotment, 7–79; language, 59, 93, 141, 149–150; livestock, 53–54, 74, 76, 80–81; Mexican government policy toward, 80, 92–93, 96, 98; mining involvement, 75; missionization, 55–57; music, 59, 141; nomads, 15, 39; origin story, 18–19; outing program, 76–77; population, 11, 83, 91, 93, 118; pottery, 4, 87–88, 110–112; relation to other Pimans, 37; relations with Anglo-Americans, 52–53, 54–55, 73–79, 111–113; religion, 50–51, 55–57, 60, 99–106, 109, 123–124, 127, 129; rodeos, 143; salt expeditions, 99; salt trade, 73; schools, 76, 96, 122; settlements, 16, 39–41, 43, 47–48, 59; subsistence, 15–16, 39–41, 43, 45–46, 59; tribal council, 120; tribal districts, 120; types, based on subsistence, 39–41, 43, 45–46; U.S. government

ABOUT THE AUTHOR AND THE PHOTOGRAPHER

For the past thirty-three years, author Bernard L. Fontana has lived close to the western edge of the San Xavier Papago Indian Reservation. During this time, he has studied Papago history and culture and was an expert witness in the tribe's successfully prosecuted claims case against the federal government. An ethnologist and field historian at the University of Arizona, he brings warmth and an understanding to his account of contemporary Papago life.

John P. Schaefer, formerly president of the University of Arizona, is an outstanding photographer of the West. His extraordinary images capture the essence of the Papago experience as it is revealed in their faces, their homes, their churches, and the land itself: this Land of Little Rain.